We Begin Here

We Begin Here

Poems for Palestine and Lebanon

Edited by
Kamal Boullata and Kathy Engel

Interlink Books

An imprint of Interlink Publishing Group, Inc.
Northampton, Massachusetts

First published in 2007 by

INTERLINK BOOKS
An imprint of Interlink Publishing Group, Inc.
46 Crosby Street, Northampton, Massachusetts 01060
www.interlinkbooks.com

Library of Congress Cataloging-in-Publication Data
We begin here : poems for Palestine and Lebanon / edited by Kamal Boullata & Kathy Engel.
p. cm.
ISBN 978-1-56656-687-2 (pbk.)
1. American poetry—21st century. 2. Arab–Israeli conflict—Poetry. 3. Palestine–Poetry. 4. Lebanon–Poetry. I. Boullata, Kamal, 1942– II. Engel, Kathy.
PS617.W4 2007
811'.6080358—dc22
2007007431

Printed and bound in Canada by Webcom

To the memory of

Eqbal Ahmad
(1933–1999)

and

June Jordan
(1936–2002)

CONTENTS

Part Two: And Not Surrender

ACKNOWLEDGMENTS

Putting together an anthology of contemporary poetry is by definition a collective enterprise. Thanks to all the friends and colleagues who trusted in our book project and who gave so generously of their time and resources to assist us at various stages of our work. Before recognizing each one of them, we wish to express our gratitude to the Blue Mountain Center in Blue Mountain Lake, New York, where we first met in the summer of 1982. It was during our residency at the center that Israel's military invasion of Lebanon was launched and we began thinking of organizing a series of poetry readings against the invasion. A book published to accompany the readings was to become the nucleus of the present publication.

After losing contact with each other for over two decades, it was Israel's 2006 war on Lebanon that prompted us to look once again for one another. We mutually felt the need to reissue the 1982 book and expand it to include the voices of a wider chorus of poets who have been writing in response to the spiraling wars in the region.

First and foremost we wish to thank all the poets who entrusted us with the poems that make up this anthology. Their immediate and enthusiastic responses were heart-warming and their support for our project sustained us throughout our work. Thanks are also due to John Berger for the line drawing he contributed and to Aharon Shabtai and to his English translator Peter Cole, who allowed us to use extracts from "Failure" in the introduction.

We also acknowledge with thanks all those who helped us relocate poet friends we have lost contact with over the years and to those who provided us with the addresses of new poets we wished to include. Our thanks are due to Alexander Taylor of Curbstone Press, Willimantic, CT; Laurence Singer of Rhythms of the Globe, Flushing, NY; Steven Salaita of Virginia Polytechnic Institute, Blacksburgh,VA; Issa Boullata of the

Institute of Islamic Studies, McGill University, Montreal; and Olivia Zemor of Librairie Resistances, Paris. Contributing poets further helped us locate other colleagues. We warmly thank Sarah Browning, Martín Espada, Nathalie Handal, Samuel Hazo, Jack Hirschman, and E. Ethelbert Miller. In particular, thanks to Suheir Hammad for encouragement, ideas, and help reaching poets.

As for contributing poet James Scully, who never failed to answer any of Kamal's queries, his generosity as a friend, his poetry, critical acumen, and intellectual engagement have continued to be a source of inspiration. In addition, his constructive comments along with those of Arlene Scully were enlightening to Kamal's introduction. Special thanks are due to both of them.

Special thanks are also due to Melanie Kaye/Kantrowitz and Jonathan Snow, who offered generous, insightful readings of Kathy's preface. As always, Jonathan, together with Ella and Justine Engel-Snow, put up with Kathy's anxiety and distraction during the creation of a new work. Margaret Ratner's keen eye was additionally of inestimable value to Kathy. Her friendship, support, and help with key correspondence and research is particularly appreciated.

We would like to thank a number of generous friends who believed in our book project from the day we announced our intention to devote all the time required to produce it: Harriet Barlow and the Blue Mountain Center, Marsha Norman, Donna Katzin, and Jean Stein. We are deeply grateful for Hari Dillon and the Vanguard Foundation's generosity and commitment. In addition, we thank Leslie Cagan and the Media and Democracy Project of the Institute for Media Analysis and Fractured Atlas.

We wish to express deep appreciation to the following friends who responded swiftly and generously with assistance: Nadia Hijab, Dorothy Zellner, Nicole DePriest, and Kelly McAnnany. In particular, we wish to thank Lily Farhoud, whose research, editorial interventions, and administrative management throughout all stages of work on this project was a burden she assumed with good humor and matchless grace.

As this expanded anthology is going to press 24 years after its original collection was first published, it is with joy that one remembers the commitment of special friends who lent wings to the publication of the first edition. They include Claudette Shwiry, executive director of the Arab American Cultural Foundation, who had facilitated all avenues to expedite the realization of that edition and the organization of the poetry readings; Nuha T. Alhegelan for her generosity and support of both projects; and Eqbal Ahmad and Mirène Ghossein, each of whom helped in more ways than they have known.

As for the present edition, we would like to thank Phyllis Bennis of the Institute for Policy Studies in Washington, D.C., for suggesting to us that we contact Michel Moushabeck, publisher and editor of Interlink Publishing, who instantly saw the importance of this work. We extend our thanks to Michel and to all members of his staff at the press for bringing this book to light.

Finally, thanks are due to Ramzi Haidar, whose photograph, appearing on the cover, served as a compass for Kamal since he first saw it until the completion of his work on the anthology. It captures a Palestinian refugee woman, living in Lebanon since 1948, meeting for the first time a family relative on the Lebanese–Israeli border in 2000.

If the message relayed by our book succeeds in reaching an audience, it is due to the collective involvement of individuals who believed all along that aesthetic expression could be formidable when its articulation is inseparable from the struggle for political justice and social change.

—Kamal Boullata and Kathy Engel

PREFACE

One of the reasons I have come to concentrate on imagination as a means through which we can assemble a coherent world is that imagination is what, above all, makes empathy possible.

—Maxine Greene
Releasing the Imagination

We begin here. In the space between words. Our multilingual sounds affirm presence, conscience, memory. Community. Poems from 1982. From 2006. Same wars. Same occupations. Before, during, still. More poets. More voices acting as bodies in resistance.

As the bombs shatter vision—voices blurred, ears blocked, homes exploded, history erased—we ask ourselves what we can do. Sign statements, stand in streets. We do. Some put bodies in the way of bulldozers. Some lobby. Some knock on doors. We hold one another through our words. We are writers. Our vocation is to gather the stories in languages we must keep alive, hoping they can, in some sense, save lives.

We begin here. Some of us have family living under occupation, living with war. Others of us imagine from what seems a safe distance, living in the place that pays for the danger and reconfigures the stories. In July, I received a message that was widely distributed through the internet, from a post-Hurricane Katrina volunteer, now working in Lebanon, saying something like: "Let the Lebanese and Palestinian people know there are those in the United States who care; they are not alone. Let them know."

Throughout my adult life I had heard this message again and again. From mothers in Nicaragua and El Salvador. Rwanda. Haiti. From a man standing beside his bulldozed home in Gaza. From those in this country who have been violated. I have learned that this humble showing of concern and connection carries meaning, holds light.

This book is our way of reaching our arms to the people living in terror in Lebanon and Occupied Palestine, to let them know that we will not be silent. Letting the people in the U.S. and the world know. We send these words into the world, together, in multiple tongues, pasts, and perceptions, the way one plants seeds in the earth, to counter the terror with growing. We offer our tools.

We begin here with what we have—ourselves—and what we imagine and make—these poems. We make them in silence and in raucous clamor, letter by letter, breath by holding breath—incarcerated, in a field, reaching through barbed wire across a border surrounded by armed guards, or by a glistening lake, loons swooping above; in cluster fire, on cement streets. We make our art in relation to one another—what we can control and what is beyond our capacity—the geography of living and dying. The poems are made of love and human utterance. Frailty and unfathomable tenacity. They can't bring back the dead but they keep us alive, and they live because they manifest and extend our selves, our souls, our faith. They enter the world and stay like molecules floating through the air. Made from thought, daring, complex and historic love, everyday life, a desire for truth and the will to remember, these poems are necessary. They are medicine, muscle, bones, and they are laughter. They are wit when it seems there can be none. These works, born of our individual and collective spirits and minds, born of our tentative bodies, represent our capacity to question, to survive, to become, stretch toward sovereignty of mind and heart, toward one another, living in dissonance, reaching for wholeness.

The poems and all that they're made of cross over lines dividing families and groups of families with names that are linguistically related. Syntax reaches through prison bars. Even after shards of metal burn flesh and tanks crush living rooms, there's a chance the thinking, daring love endures, the song prevails. Hopefully, but not always. Sometimes lives are ruined by brutality from which we cannot recover. But the words leak through. This book comes to us the way life comes—through the torment and resilience of memory, alchemy, the miracle of some of us still being here.

We name ourselves after places, Gods and Goddesses, fantasy, something we call history. We each eat food, drink liquid, need to be held, breathe air, take care of our children, take care of our parents, look for tomorrow, stand in today. Each. We are not policies. We are not borderlines. We are not territories. We are not passports or identity cards. We are not walls. We are not untranslatable. We are not bulldozers. We are not occupations. We are not representatives. We are not less than human. We are daughters and sons, mothers and fathers, sisters and brothers and cousins, grandparents, people looking for what can be shared.

We are Gaza, New Orleans, Hebron, Baghdad, Haifa, Lydda. We are New York, Texas, Paris, Oklahoma, Soweto, Beirut, Rwanda, Warsaw, Grenada, Ramallah, Haiti, Darfur, Vietnam, Bethlehem. We are Jerusalem. We are the places I haven't named and the people we haven't met. We are world wars and civil wars. Families and shattered families. We are 1943. 1948. 1967. We are 1982, 2001, 2003, 2006, and all the other years. We are survivors of crimes against our humanity, and sometimes we are the criminals, amnesiac, complicit with crimes. We are sleepwalkers, carriers of nightmares. We are dreamers, carriers of hope.

We begin here. We are Kamal in France and Kathy in New York, out of touch for more than two decades, finding one another once again amidst the news of horror, to make a gift. We are each poet in this book, identities rooted in making. We transgress national borders and religious restrictions, fascinated with cultural practice. Our identities re-examine what it means to be human, what we mean when we say freedom. When we say bread, school, health. When we say love, other. When we say truth, survival, respect. What it means to attempt to feel what another feels, see what another sees. We write for the possible.

We are strangers who meet seeking peace. Together we become a haiku, a sonnet, a villanelle, a family of poems yearning to give something back to the shattered spirit of the world, yearning for wholeness, to do our part in imagining our humanity more tender. Without this imagining we cannot conceive of change. We know that our silence would sentence us. We know that what happens in the ancient cultures and land called the Middle East touches every life on earth. We know the power of a word, a name. Palestine.

What we have to offer is the word that can't be erased in any language.

Each poem gracing the pages of this volume records and challenges what is, adjusts what can be.

Olive. Cedar of Lebanon. Oil. Ash. Earth. Sun. Light. Family. Neighbor.

What one sees that no one saw before. What one sees that we all see. How one tells it.

We begin here. We make these poems, imperfect, finding our way, in gratitude, in reverence, in grief and resistance, building, for places and people, ashes to breath, for Palestine, for Lebanon, for meaning, for all of us.

—Kathy Engel

Sagaponack, New York
January 16, 2007

INTRODUCTION

Susan Sontag writes: "No 'we' should be taken for granted when the subject is looking at other people's pain." In these poems, written in response to the serial wars ravaging the peoples of the Middle East, the "we" is as much "them" as it is "us." If, due to our safe distance from the war zones, we fail "to hold this reality in mind," it's not because we're different people with different ethnic or national identities, but that we lack basic human "imagination [and] empathy."[1]

Empathy, or "creative understanding" as Bakhtin has it, is not simply an emotional reflection that mirrors others' circumstances, or that totally "identifies" with the other.[2] The witness maintains his or her own ground. The other is always other. There is an ineluctable degree of separation between the two. In similar terms, translators of literary texts are expected to find "a middle ground" between "identification" with the voice in the alien or source language and maintaining a "critical distance" from it.[3]

In the present volume composed of two parts, Part I includes the most recent poems written in response to the ongoing wars in the Middle East. In Part II, the reader finds the reprinting of the collection of poems written in response to

1 Susan Sontag, *Regarding the Pain of Others*, (London, Penguin Books, 2004), 6, 7.

2 According to Webster's *New World Dictionary* the current meaning of empathy, which implies "intellectual identification with another," comes into English from the Greek *empatheia* and the German *Einfühlung*—a late 19th- century translation of the Greek term originally composed of the prefix "in" and the word for "pathos." Both Greek and German terms shared a common meaning that literally translates to "feeling in," but the Greek word, employed as the opposite of apathy, implied an ethical connotation, whereas the German translation was used to define the aesthetic response of identifying with the subject of a literary product or a work of art. See David Depew, "Empathy, Psychology, and Aesthetics: Reflections on a Repair Concept," *Poroi* 4, no. 1, March 2004. (inpress.lib.uiowa.edu/poroi/papers/depew050301.html).

By merging the ethical and the aesthetic applications, M.M. Bakhtin proposed an alternative concept based on the Russian neologism *vzhivanie*, or "living into": "to enter actively into another individuality, another perspective on the world—without losing sight, even momentarily, of one's own unique perspective, one's own 'surplus' of life experience, one's own sense of self." Gary Saul Morson and Caryl Emerson, *Mikhail Bakhtin: Creation of a Prosaics* (Stanford, CA: Stanford University Press,1990) 53–54. Quoted in Russell Scott Valentino, "The Oxymoron of Empathic Criticism: Readerly Empathy, Critical Explication and the Translator's Creative Understanding." *Poroi* 4, no. 1, March 2005, 15 (inpress.lib.uiowa.edu/poroi/papers/valentino050301). In later writings, Bakhtin referred to the dialogical concept he coined simply as "creative understanding."

3 Ibid. Valentino, 14.

the 1982 Israeli invasion of Lebanon—in particular, to the Sabra and Shatila massacres. These earliest poems were made public, for the first time, in three readings that Sara Miles, Kathy Engel, and I helped organize for our poet friends. The Arab American Cultural Foundation in Washington, D.C., sponsored these events, and Congressman John Conyers hosted them to capacity audiences at New York's Ethical Culture Auditorium and the Detroit Institute of Arts. The third reading, presented at the Rayburn Building on Capitol Hill, was a unique occasion. It was, and still is, the only time that a member of Congress welcomed a group of American poets, within congressional premises, to read poems protesting a war supported by the US government.

To accompany this series of readings I put together a selection of the poems in a modest anthology that took its title from a poem by Sara Miles. *And Not Surrender: American Poets on Lebanon* (1982) has long been out of print. Reproduced here in Part II, it marks the beginning of what would become, within two decades, a broader chorus of American voices protesting the wars that continue to devastate the Middle East, with mounting numbers of civilian victims killed, maimed, impoverished, and dispossessed.

As for the poems found in Part I, they are mostly written in response to the Israeli assault on Lebanon during the summer of 2006. These include, as well, poems in reaction to the US invasion of Iraq. Its title is taken from Lawrence Ferlinghetti's "Speak Out," a poem widely circulated in 2003. At that time Sam Hamill, having declined an invitation to read at the White House, launched a genuinely democratic campaign to organize both established and aspiring American poets of all ages and circumstances to speak out on the US war in Iraq. For the first time since the Vietnam War, this campaign recaptured the groundswell of general, non-academic interest in poetry. Hundreds of poetry readings were held across the country. The poets' message was once again taken to Washington. In March 2003, Hamill and W.S. Merwin, joined by Terry Tempest Williams, presented members of Congress at the Longworth House Office Building with a document containing more than

13,000 anti-war poems that had been submitted to the *Poets Against War* website.[4]

Most poems in this collection address the two US-backed wars waged by Israel on neighboring Lebanon. Even so, poems responding to the plight of the Palestinian people, an issue that has virtually governed political events in the region before and after the two wars, continue to track the undercurrent running through, and linking, both sections of the anthology. Borders created and policed by Israel have separated villagers and family members from each other, and farmers from their orchards and fields. At the same time the calamities visited on the Lebanese and the Palestinian people on both sides of the borders have, over the decades, only deepened their bonds. Historically and objectively, the destiny of one becomes inseparable from the destiny of the other.

In the 1982 invasion of Lebanon, which culminated with the Israeli siege of Beirut and the Sabra and Shatila massacres, more than 20,000 Palestinians and Lebanese were killed over a four-month period, and thousands more were wounded. Lebanon's infrastructure was totally destroyed. Palestinian fighters were driven out of Beirut. Institutions serving Palestinian refugee camps—schools, hospitals, small businesses, and cultural centers—were reduced to rubble.[5]

Two decades later, during 34 days in July and August of 2006, Israel fired on a daily basis between 3,000 and 6,000 bombs, rockets and artillery rounds, killing over 1,200 Lebanese civilians including hundreds of children, and wounding over 4,000. Homes, offices, apartment buildings were leveled; hospitals, supermarkets, churches, and mosques were struck. Bridges, power plants and their fuel tanks were bombed as a sea and air blockade was imposed on Lebanon.[6] Meanwhile,

4 Sam Hamill informed me in his September 2, 2006, email that John Conyers and Maxine Waters were among the representatives who welcomed the three poets on Capitol Hill. In his September 23, 2006, letter to me, W.S. Merwin denounced "the maltreatment, injustice and devastation currently being visited upon the Palestinian and Lebanese people, by the American-supplied Israelis, … In 1982 I felt the same way and found few people who shared my grief and outrage."
5 For an eyewitness report of the 1982 invasion of Lebanon see Chris Giannou, *Beseiged: A Doctor's Story of Life and Death in Beirut*, (Northampton, MA: Olive Branch Press, 1992.) For a more comprehensive background, see Robert Fisk, *Pity the Nation: The Abduction of Lebanon*, 4th ed. (New York: Nation Books, 2002).
6 See the report of the UN Mine Action Coordination Center (UNMACC) "South Lebanon: Cluster Bomb Info Sheet," November 4, 2006. See also Amnesty International, "Israel/Lebanon: Out of all Proportions, Civilians Bear the Brunt of the War," November 21, 2006 (AI Index: MDE 02/033/2006).

America's closest ally in the region continued punitive bombing raids on civilian targets in the Gaza Strip, one of the most densely populated areas in the world. A starvation blockade backed by the US (which shut off all Palestinian access to global financial institutions) was imposed on the population.

Israeli historian Ilan Pappé wrote that "the Lebanese war provided a fog for a while, covering over the war crimes in the Gaza Strip," a region sealed off from the world, an open-air prison where "a genocide" and an "ethnic cleansing policy" was underway. He added: the "daily business of slaying Palestinians, many of them children, is now reported in the internal pages of the local press, quite often in microscopic fonts."[7] Even after "at least 37 civilians" were killed within four days in Beit Hanoun, it was reported "Israeli public opinion yawns with indifference."[8]

Concurrently, the Israeli poet Aharon Shabtai articulated the courage of Israelis who refused to serve in Israel's wars or in its occupied territories. In a poem emblazoned "Failure," on the heels of the Israeli assault on Lebanon, he wrote: I pray/ for the failure/ of this// stinking war.// Spread your wings/ and come, merciful failure/ come.// ...// In the name of the beautiful/ books I've read—// in the name of the kisses / I've kissed—// may the army be vanquished.// ...// In this war// I'm for/ the villages,// for the mosques// ...// In this war// I'm for/ the Shi'ite family// for Tyre//...// for the mother/ the grandfather// for the eight/ kids in the minivan,// for the white/ silk kerchief..."[9]

Continents away, American poets responded to Israel's massive killings of Lebanese and Palestinian civilians with an empathy grounded in the same humanitarian realization as that of Aharon Shabtai. Their diverse background experiences and contrasting sensibilities disclose a wide range of styles and techniques: from the confessional lyric to the linear narrative, with some poems written in a formal social language and others ringing with more colloquial expression. There is verse that springs from imaginative projection, and the witness poetry whose images and stories are derived, more often than not, from

7 Ilan Pappé, "Genocide in Gaza," International Middle East Media Center, September 4, 2006 (www.imemc.org/article/21248). See also his "Palestine 2007: Genocide in Gaza, Ethnic Cleansing in the West Bank" in the Electronic Intifada, January 11, 2007. (www.electronicintifada.net/v2/article6374.shtml)

8 *Haaretz*, November 6, 2006.

9 Shabtai's verses are extracted from stanzas 1, 4, 7–9 of "Failure," translated from the Hebrew by Peter Cole and first published in *Eleven Eleven*.

TV images, journals, and news reports. Side by side each poem sets a different level of reflection and feeling—each with its unique burden of accumulated information—to emerge as a chorus of voices: concerted personal notes of empathy for, and occasionally solidarity with, the plight and the struggles of people living in Palestine, Lebanon, and Iraq.

In reality, the American poets' own sense of humanity could only find its full expression in relation to the "other." By embracing peoples living beyond the borders of the American continent, American poets present us here with a body of literature that testifies they are "living into" the promise and principles of the multicultural society America pledged as a nation. It is no coincidence that the earliest poems in the present anthology were first heard in the halls of the US Congress.

Which of these urgently written poems will survive, only future critics can tell. But if poems from 1982 have resonance to poetry written during the Vietnam War, and certain images from that time can still be interchanged with those evoked by events in 2006, then we have an indication that as long as state-sponsored wars continue to be waged against civilians, this poetry will not cease to be relevant, and its images will continue to have life. It will survive beyond all the daily-televised newsbreaks and newspaper reports that have gone spinning into the void of the last forty years.

In any case, the "aesthetic understanding" awakened by the imagination of the poets remains barren until, transpired through the space between page and reader, it is realized. For us, as readers, here is where we begin.

—Kamal Boullata

Menton, France
January 19, 2007

PART ONE

Speak Out

2006

After 'Guernica' (1937) — Beirut, Cana, Tyr (2006)

Lawrence Ferlinghetti

Speak Out

And a vast paranoia sweeps across the land
And America turns the attack on its Twin Towers
Into the beginning of the Third World War
The war with the Third World

And the terrorists in Washington
Are shipping out the young men
To the killing fields again

And no one speaks

And they are rousting out
All the ones with turbans
And they are flushing out
All the strange immigrants

And they are shipping all the young men
To the killing fields again

And no one speaks

And when they come to round up
All the great writers and poets and painters
The National Endowment of the Arts of Complacency
Will not speak

While all the young men
Will be killing all the young men
In the killing fields again

So now is the time for you to speak
All you lovers of liberty
All you lovers of the pursuit of happiness

All you lovers and sleepers
Deep in your private dream
Now is the time for you to speak
O silent majority
Before they come for you!

Grace Cavalieri

How a Poem Begins

It's a little thing. Could be
the long O's in Kosovo, or
a woman
alone in the street
after the hurricane
sweeping Honduras,
the sound of the wind
in New Orleans, or
the rubble of Lebanon.
They say poetry is insignificant,
such a tiny voice
no one can hear.
That's why we write of such
little things, insignificant things.

Margaret Gibson

Tracks

2 p.m.: Strong sun. The convoy has stalled
on the road to Debel. Far off, flecks of light
from a town as yet intact

As when a man goes so deep into the history of his pain
it becomes the only dream
he can remember behind his dark glasses

As when the diplomats speak, everything as clear
as sun on a broken towing cable.

Nothing moves. In the press car, the Archbishop of Tyre
clad in a cassock of salt

2 o'clock: the ground is scored with tank tracks

the invasion of Lebanon
August 6, 2006
(after Tomas Transtromer)

James Scully

Qana*

where the wedding was
where water turned to wine
where the best was saved
for last

shsh   they're trying to sleep
in the dark wood
of dreamless dreaming—
coughing farting snoring sighing
turning over

where the wedding was
the rolling storm
that is not a storm
flies over

it doesn't feel much
to drop a bomb—
a slight bump
under the wing

the thing is done—

their deaths
like little yapping dogs
rush out
into the nerve-endings of the universe

the bodies stay put,
impossibly still

so it was said in school
Macbeth doth murder sleep—
with so much life to kill
there's no room for sleep

in Qana
where the wedding was
those who sleep, die

the future of sleep
is buried alive

in Qana where the wedding was
the murdered in their sleep
wake just long enough to die
to become the woods
where the wedding was . . .

they are on the move now,
which is impossible

these impossible dead
growing out of their deaths
into an army of trees

* *Thought by some to be the biblical Cana. Modern Qana is the site of two massacres—the first in 1996, when Israeli shelling killed 106 sleeping refugees in a UN compound. Ten years later, on 30 July 2006, the Israelis bombed a basement shelter where Lebanese citizens were sleeping. Of the 56 people killed, 34 were children. The bomb, a laser-controlled BSU 37/B 'bunker buster' with a depleted uranium (DU) warhead, was supplied by the US.*

IAF General Dan Halutz: "What do I feel when I drop a bomb? A slight bump in the airplane." Adding: "By the way, I sleep well at night."

The Israeli military reported that the Hizbullah-led Lebanese resistance used trees to camouflage rocket launchers. A cedar tree, symbolic of Lebanon, appears on the national flag.

Sam Hamod

Shredding Innocence

for Lebanon, its people, its villages and those who tried to flee Marwaheen

Her mother
screaming, "Ya Allah, Ya Allah..."
her father,
bleeding beside his limp daughter,
his arm
over her, where he'd
tried covering her
when the F16 struck,
shall we speak of the Israeli bullhorns
blaring in the bright morning sunlight,
"Evacuate, get out of Marwaheen,
get out if you wish to live,
get out!"
shall we speak of the well-meaning
UN observers, who urged them
to climb into the old trucks, wagons
and cars, to head up the road
to Beirut, to save themselves,
or shall we speak of the F16s
swooping down
on this helpless convoy,
rockets and guns blazing,
donkeys and trucks bursting
into air, of people jumping
out of cars and backs
of trucks, when the planes came back
for a second run, strafing,
blood, shall we speak of blood, that
red life force oozing out
from each single body,
of the screaming like the planes,

of the same blood
that was shed by other villages,
ghosted by Israeli tanks and bulldozers,
after the Israeli planes and helicopters
tore them apart
like this riddled young body,
shredded,
this innocent girl—
though you may say
she is not mine,
nor is she yours,
but I know, she is ours,
she is part of what we are,
what we have allowed,
in the dust of the road,
where the truck still burns,
this sweet bleeding rag doll of a girl
tears at my heart

Andy Young

Thinking of Rasha, of Beirut

Santa Fe, July 14, 2006

It's raining in the desert
as bombs
                                        fall on Beirut

a small tidy square on my screen
                                        shows smoke
                                        billowing up from the airport

firecrackers sweets
                          in the streets
to the south

where they vow to fight back
                          already your ship is burning
                          already your ship sinks into the sea

nuts and drips
of honey

            cordite and blood

the world in shock

            you've been forgotten
you'd told me, New Orleans
was shocking, and then it was forgotten

                                        will it be the same for you?

last week
            you wrote of your worry

for Gaza

and I dreamt all night
of flying there
trying to gather my lover my father
where were our passports? would they work?
which airport where exactly *is* the war?

I search the news:
another man walking through fire
another man holding a limp child another another

the story of Hatem Attar whose cousins
were killed for giving sandbags to their neighbors
to protect them from bullets. Outside their funeral
he says:
I'm against firing Qassams into Israel,
but if I had a houseful of Qassams right now,
I'd fire them all into Israel

no word from you for two days
power cut when bombs hit
city center

I wonder where exactly you live

your last note: *write to me I feel*
less isolated

how do I send this

how do I ask you where
people go when their houses are dust

where you should stand
when the floor shakes

if
you think we survive

because we must:
stubborn shrubs
in the desert

grateful for,
drinking in
the rain?

Naomi Shihab Nye

Letters My Prez is Not Sending

Dear Rafik, Sorry about that soccer game
you won't be attending since you now
have no...

Dear Fawziya, You know, I have a mom too
so I can imagine what you...

Dear Shadiya, Think about your father
versus democracy, I'll bet you'd pick...

No, no, Sami, that's not true
what you said at the rally,
that our country hates you,
we really support your move
toward freedom,
that's why you no longer have
a house or a family or a village...

Dear Hassan, If only you could see
the bigger picture...

Dear Mary, I'm surprised you have
what we would call a Christian name
since you yourself...

Dear Ribhia, Sorry about that heart attack,
I know it must have been rough to live
your entire life under brutal occupation,
we're just sending a few more bombs over now
to fortify your oppressors but someday
we hope for peace in the region...
Sorry you won't be there to see it...

Dear Suheir, Surely a voice is made to be raised,
that's why we admire how you have been speaking up
but don't you see we are also speaking up
for your own interests...

Dear Sharif, Violence is wrong
unless we are using it,
why doesn't that make sense...

Dear Nadia, I did not know about
your special drawer, you know I like
to keep a few things too that have meaning to me...

Dear Ramzi, You really need to stop crying now
and go on about your business...

Dear Daddo, I know 5 kids
must feel like a lot to lose in one swoop
but we can't stop our efforts...

Dear Fatima, Of course I have feelings
for your own people, my college roommate
was from Lebanon...

Dear Mahmoud, I would answer your letter
but you must understand I still
have all those people I'm not answering in Iraq.

Andy Young

News from Beirut

on day five you write: *a quiet night in Beirut,*
more or less, compared to the night
the inhabitants of Tyre and the south
and the Beqaa and Tripoli experienced

on day six:
port of Tripoli bombed, port of Beirut bombed

the range of targets expanded to new zones of hurt:
civilians, civilians, civilians

reservoirs of fuel   piles of mint and pomegranates

⁜

we planned visits to each others' cities

you loved New Orleans, said
                    if you could
you'd live here for a while,
                              and I told you
there was always something
that drew me to Beirut—
                    the books the songs
the name itself, the "root" sound maybe

we spoke of the something that lives
in a city, that gives it mortality

you said
          try to come soon

⁜

after the flood a woman in New Orleans
was given an ammunition box
full of old love letters—they'd floated
three blocks away, the only thing to survive

what should we put in our bullet boxes
to save from flood, from rubble—
            a poem, a letter, a knife?

⁜

on the highway outside Jerusalem,
a man heads in one direction, a cart
piled high with white eggs
in the other: a truck
filled with bombs
                to fire at Lebanon

⁜

                I have to admit,
I am enduring siege with bad hair.

⁜

The roster of martyrs of this war now includes poor
soldiers, you write, *reservists who were stationed in their posts,*
watching idly the country go up in flames

I read in the *Iliad*:
"the god of war is impartial: he hands out
  death to the man who hands out death"

⁜

on day seven you say the shelling hasn't
stopped
                just more
                        blank spaces
                now

⁜

what do they need to see before they cease their fire
you ask, try to understand *the consensus*
that agrees to watch Lebanon burn

⁜

Hector's father asked Achilles to halt
the battle so he could bury his son

Achilles, who killed
Hector, agrees, then invites him to supper—

3,000 years:
we kill, we bury, we eat

we wait like Hector's wife
not knowing the battle's lost

⁜

black-shirted fighters count the dead
separate bodies from stone

but fire keeps raining
& the wind from the cyclone
of helicopter blades

⁜

during the flood, a friend drifted
on a piece of fence all night
he felt things
bumping past, took a picture,
wrapped his camera back
into its plastic bag, later
saw himself in the cemetery,

all the bodies having risen up
around him thick with water—
we spoke of our cities as ports
as places rising from dust
now our common language is death

⁂

stillness turns a corner
moves through neighborhoods

every gesture incomplete
familiar objects unfamiliar

war time mornings war time noons
siege time Beirut siege time sunsets
every dream a snarl

⁂

hero fighters claim victories
on television
when the generator works

cheers go up
in the coffee shop
where breaking news marks
the passage of time

⁂

a week into it, given a chance
to ride in a car to Damascus, you ask
for time to think:

I decided to stay. I don't know when I will
have another opportunity to leave

but, you wrote
they will not drive me away

I think of a friend in New Orleans who swam
past billboards, was left for a week at the port,
then came back as quickly as he could

dementia creeps in at the rate of news flashes
you say you fear nighttime, believe the shelling
will get worse when darkness comes *but it's not true—*
the shelling is just as intense during the day

in May you groped your way down
my stairwell, telling me in Beirut
you all keep flashlights
in your bags *just in case*

Alexis De Veaux

When Earth Is

(to those who have abused our humanity)

This shaking keeps me steady. I should know
What falls away is always. And is near.
—Theodore Roethke, *"The Waking"* (1953)

When Earth is
fed up, she will come
from the Atlantic
a hurricane, this sea of bones
once daughter
mother
braid
handprint
breath
moans these bones
beneath her
beneath her
sacred
still;

She will take those
we give to war
as spoils of arrogance
bodies come ashore
in our tears
ravaged
revengeful
our tears, cannot water
memories of trees;

Or cleanse
nightmare from daylight
a loudness of dreaming

what we owe
as above, so below;

listen
listen
when Earth quakes
beneath the sea
elephant
and bird
and snake, tremble;

these two legs
have shackled the moon
disappeared the horizon;

When Earth is fed up
even fish will chant, beware
words of a street prophet:
your chickens
have come home
to roost

Richard Schaaf

No Natural Disaster

No time to think
where they're going
what they're running to

We're running too
dropping everything

conversation
coffee the newspaper
thoughts
work
the day's plans

the rest of our lives

running fast faster
than anyone can think

it's unthinkable
to think

just running
running

from no
natural disaster

Lawrence Ferlinghetti

Dragon's Teeth

A headless man is running
down the street
He is carrying his head
in his hands
A woman runs after him
She has his heart
in her hands
The bombs keep falling
sowing hate
And they keep running
down the streets
Not the same two people
but thousands of others & brothers
All running
from the bombs that keep falling
sowing pure hate

And for every bomb that's dropped
up spring a thousand Bin Ladens
a thousand new terrorists
Like dragon's teeth sown
From which armed warriors sprang up
Crying for blood

As the smart bombs sowing hate
Keep falling and falling and falling

E. Ethelbert Miller

For Lebanon

Why is there always a sequel to madness?

We are running out of wars
We ran out of peace a long time ago

Only people are running
No one is running out of bullets and bombs

The world is miming on empty
We are doing nothing

We must surrender to love
Once again we must surrender

Is there nothing under our nakedness?

Nathalie Handal

At the End of a Cedar Tree

I

The sea birds of Beirut tell them:
Here we worship the breeze.

And I ask:

When will you leave our tree-songs alone?

Stop living off the proceeds of Hafiz and Rumi,
translating our history to suit your needs?

When will you leave our seasons
dancing in old squares in Damascus or Beirut alone?

When will you release our silver shadows
amber reverie, tortured prisoners?

When will we stop holding water in our mouth,
stop praying for rain, the absence of moonlight?

When will we stop lighting one candle after another
waahid, itnein, talaata, arbaa, khamsa, sitta,
stop at one hundred for now. Ahmad Jabour. Seven.

When will we stop saying that death is warm
for the room we've spent our entire life in
has frozen our limbs?

When will bullets stop hiding in our books,
the staircases we once flirted in?

When will your generals and lords
leave us to our coffee, our view?

When will we see our cities again?

When I ask, will you stop
telling us to walk to our freedom
leave our homes
take a boat?

When will the wolves leave,
and why does
only silence have a tongue?

II

When will I stop driving through I-95
wondering why I'm here, stop
reading *Vogue*, thinking of September's
fashion statement, pretend we recycle
and forget New Orleans happened.

And where is all the Jazz, our brothers in Harlem,
America's stream boats, old records
dirty handkerchiefs?

Don't you understand, we are the people of the sea,
we swim with blue and yellow fishes,
eat peaches and apricots,
and you keep standing in our way
blocking our towns while
smuggling our music and anything else you can.

Don't you see, you have lost.
Despite your Lucky cigarettes and swords.
Despite the farmlands you continue to steal
and Jerusalem you try to keep away from us.

Our hearts might be dizzy with the
smell of blood, our balconies empty, but

our rusted roofs will never
stop being rose fields
our cafes never stop singing
our blue mosques never stop raising.

We will no longer be your hostage?
But I still have to ask,
have you forgotten what it is to be American
or perhaps you've realized
that we actually found lightning
and black maps, the Mississippi river
and the corn fields of Iowa,
the silence of Oklahoma
and the dates of Sidon, the words of
Langston Hughes and that of lamp-carrier,
the recital of water-stones and angel-bird
at the end of a cedar tree…
I hear the birds of Beirut. Do you?

Joy Harjo

Equinox

I must keep from breaking into the story by force,
If I do I will find a war club in my hand
And the smoke of grief staggering toward the sun,
Your nation dead beside you.

I keep walking away though it has been an eternity
And from each drop of blood
Springs up sons and daughters, trees
A mountain of sorrows, of songs.

I tell you this from the dusk of a small city in the north
Not far from the birthplace of cars and industry.
Geese are returning to mate and crocuses have
Broken through the frozen earth.

Soon they will come for me and I will make my stand
Before the jury of destiny. Yes, I will answer in the clatter
Of the new world, I have broken my addiction to war
And desire. Yes, I will reply, I have buried the dead

And made songs of the blood, the marrow.

Saladin Ahmed

Libra in Times of War

So much of my life has been defined
by the inability to make decisions—
at nine years old, Haji put it before me:
Heaven or Hell, belief or disbelief,
a toy robot? A video game?

Now in the spring-like sweat of Midtown on the edge,
planes explode over weeks and mountains,
commentators get things wrong,
and I am asked to choose:
quiet or loud,
apocalypse or apocalypse.

There is a party a train ride away,
a booty call and a drink Uptown,
a stack of books to study while the neighbors argue.

I have spent so much time on street corners,
looking confused and intent—
it has been seventeen years!

There is a glowing screen,
a bit of black dress-trim and golden skin,
regrets shaped like lions with sandstorms in their throats.

It is warmer than it has ever been beyond my birthday
and I am thinking about terrorists and empires,
craft and vision, ancestors and fat.
There is Semtex and a beauty mark and my heart,
reawakened by something in the air—
love? Anthrax?

Susan Sherman

Here's a Poem

to the poets who die unknown
who live their poems day by day
bare the chaos of lost words
Here's to the poems that never get published
that lie fallow in someone's veins
that burned in Hiroshima and Nagasaki Vietnam
New York City Portland, Maine
Here's to the poets in Nicaragua
Cuba South Africa El Salvador
in the southern countryside of all the Americas
and the northern cities too
Here's to the women and men
who never even knew they were poets
had no one to tell them
didn't know how to tell themselves
Here's to the millions of words buried in a
million places all over the globe
the mouths and hands silenced forever
Here's to all that magic music beauty
surprise that died unsung that dies everyday
that blood that moves us forward
that holds back the tide

Dennis Brutus

In this time in this air
to live is to be saddened
awareness of pain is
pervasive as the air
each labored death draws
from a miasma of sorrow
the ribcage creaks pain
expelling, not expunging sadness:
still falls the rain of horror
the landscape is drenched with destruction:
"business as usual" goes the cry,
business of profits, of death and dying
how goes the world away
how goes the business of war

Sarah Browning

Sunday Outing with Yellow Leaves

In November of our first year here we took our son walking
in Rock Creek Park. War hung like the clacking helicopters
everywhere—and fear. Ben had already been to three demonstrations,
knew the dull repetition of speeches and chants, knew the
closed faces of cops.

He was still just four and we wondered each day
what we had done, bringing him here. In the park
yellow leaves clung to the ash. The brown oak
rattled as we brushed past on the high paths. *Mommy!*
Ben announced, *Today I'm the teacher!*

Follow the teacher, boys and girls—he knew the tone of grown-ups
everywhere—waving the yellow flag of an enormous leaf
he had found, running off, ahead. I stopped to watch
another helicopter clack clack above. I worried about the slick
dry leaves on the steep path, I worried about the hidden rocks.

Now, a year has passed and we, of course, have survived this war.
Others, who have not, are mourned by mothers thousands of miles
from here and five miles from here. Helicopters still racket the skies,
but I am used to them. Months pass between demonstrations.
We read our poems of resistance. We know
we will be marching forever. We live here now.

Samuel Hazo

Suffer the Little Children

Just four months into history,
  Sarah speaks in the key of squeaks
  while reaching for her rattle.
                                        Nothing
  distracts her but a televised explosion
  and screams before her father
  mutes the screen.
                              The screams
  sound louder in silence.
                                    Powdered
  by bombdust, remnants
  of children litter a street
  in Qana,
                    Rescuers bundle
  Bits and bodies in oriental
  rugs for burial,
                              I turn
  away to gaze at Sarah
  sucking on her rattle.
                                  As image
  overlaps with image, bombdust
  seems to whiten her cheeks.
I make a face to see
  if she will laugh.
                              She waits
  until my face becomes my face
  again, then blooms into a grin.
The silence keeps on screaming.

Adrienne Rich

The School Among the Ruins

Beirut. Baghdad. Sarajevo. Bethlehem. Kabul.
Not of course here.

1
Teaching the first lesson and the last
—great falling light of summer will you last
longer than schooltime?

When children flow
in columns at the doors
BOYS GIRLS and the busy teachers

open or close high windows
with hooked poles drawing darkgreen shades

closets unlocked, locked
questions unasked, asked, when

love of the fresh impeccable
sharp-pencilled yes
order without cruelty

a street on earth neither heaven nor hell
busy with commerce and worship
young teachers walking to school

fresh bread and early-open foodstalls

2
When the offensive rocks the sky when nightglare
misconstrues day and night when lived-in

rooms from the upper city
tumble cratering lower streets

cornices of olden ornament human debris
when fear vacuums out the streets

When the whole town flinches
blood on the undersole thickening to glass

Whoever crosses hunched knees bent a contested zone
knows why she does this suicidal thing

School's now in session day and night
children sleep
in the classrooms teachers rolled close

3
How the good teacher loved
his school the students
the lunchroom with fresh sandwiches

lemonade and milk
the classroom glass cages
of moss and turtles
teaching responsibility

A morning breaks without bread or fresh-poured milk
parents or lesson-plans

diarrhea first question of the day
children shivering it's September
Second question: where is my mother?

4
One: I don't know where your mother
is Two: I don't know
why they are trying to hurt us
Three: or the latitude and longitude
of their hatred Four: I don't know if we
hate them as much I think there's more toilet paper
in the supply closet I'm going to break it open

Today this is your lesson:
write as clearly as you can
your name home street and number
down on this page
No you can't go home yet
but you aren't lost
this is our school

I'm not sure what we'll eat
we'll look for healthy roots and greens
searching for water though the pipes are broken

5
There's a young cat sticking
her head through window bars
she's hungry like us

but can feed on mice
her bronze erupting fur
speaks of a life already wild

her golden eyes
don't give quarter She'll teach us Let's call her
Sister
when we get milk we'll give her some

6
I've told you, let's try to sleep in this funny camp
All night pitiless pilotless things go shrieking
above us to somewhere

Don't let your faces turn to stone
Don't stop asking me why
Let's pay attention to our cat she needs us

Maybe tomorrow the bakers can fix their ovens

7

"We sang them to naps told stories made
shadow-animals with our hands

washed human debris off boots and coats
sat learning by heart the names
some were too young to write
some had forgotten how"

Martín Espada

Between the Rockets and the Songs

New Year's Eve, 2003

The fireworks began at midnight,
golden sparks and rockets hissing
through the confusion of trees above our house.
I would prove to my son, now twelve,
that there was no war in the sky, not here,
so we walked down the road
to find the place where the fireworks began.
We swatted branches from our eyes,
peering at a house where the golden blaze
dissolved in smoke. There was silence,
a world of ice, then voices rose up
with the last of the sparks, singing,
and when the song showered down on us
through the leaves we leaned closer, like trees.
Rockets and singing from the same house, said my son.
We turned back down the road,
at the end of the year, at the beginning of the year,
somewhere between the rockets and the songs.

Lisa Suhair Majaj

What She Said

They don't have snow days in Palestine, they have military invasion days.
—International Solidarity Movement activists,
describing Palestinian children's lives under occupation

She said, go play outside,
but don't throw balls near the soldiers.
When a jeep goes past
keep your eyes on the ground.
And don't pick up stones,
not even for hopscotch.
She said, don't bother the neighbors;
their son was arrested last night.
Hang the laundry, make the beds,
scrub that graffiti off the walls
before the soldiers see it. She said,
there's no money; if your shoes
are too tight, cut the toes off.
This is what we have to eat;
we won't eat again until tomorrow.
No, we don't have any oranges,
they chopped down the orange trees.
I don't know why. Maybe the trees
were threatening the tanks. She said,
there's no water, we'll take baths
next week, *insha'allah.* Meanwhile,
don't flush the toilet. And don't go near
the olive grove, there are settlers there
with guns. No, I don't know how we'll harvest
the olives, and I don't know what we'll do
if they bulldoze the trees. God will provide
if He wishes, or UNRWA, but certainly not
the Americans. She said, you can't go out today,
there's a curfew. Keep away

from those windows; can't you hear
the shooting? No, I don't know why
they bulldozed the neighbor's house.
And if God knows, He's not telling.
She said, there's no school today,
it's a military invasion.
No, I don't know when it will be over,
or if it will be over. She said,
don't think about the tanks
or the planes or the guns
or what happened to the neighbors.
Come into the hallway,
it's safer there. And turn off that news,
you're too young for this. Listen,
I'll tell you a story so you won't be scared.
Kan ya ma kan—there was or there was not—
a land called *Falastine*
where children played in the streets
and in the fields and in the orchards
and picked apricots and almonds
and wove jasmine garlands for their mothers.
And when planes flew overhead
they shouted happily and waved.
Kan ya ma kan. Keep your head down.

Chris Llewellyn

Into Our

(the bombing of Baghdad, April 2003)

It's hard to believe it's the same sky to which
we raise our praising arms to warmer currents,
waking faces to take in the white brightness
blooming above the just-budded treetops.

It's hard to believe it's the same spring
rain which streams the roofs and gutters
to soak our drinking roots and growing
grasses. And it's getting harder to believe

these breezes which we breathe
have just touched the cluster
bombs, brushed countless missiles
raining fire, slicing flesh. And it's the

hardest to believe how right
now this same sky wind sun
carries the just-bloodied ones
into our water, soil, lungs.

Naomi Lazard

Elegy to the Twenty Skiers

After the accident it was clear
the pilots were zooming
through the high valley, practicing
low level flying for combat, that is, a war.
They were machine gun bullets
zapping in and out of the thin high clouds.
Maybe the twenty people trapped in the gondola
whose cable the plane snapped
because the pilot was hot-dogging—maybe
those people who fell three hundred and sixty feet
to their death, were also practicing.
In a war there are, of course, always victims,
the random selections of fate.
The only difference is this: the dead
are never informed in advance
their participation is necessary.

Richard Schaaf

Actually

Actually not
American warplanes
dropping
bombs

Actually
American airliners
bombs
actually

History of the Airplane

(Music: US National Anthem at half-speed)

And the Wright brothers said they thought they had invented
something that could make peace on earth
(if the wrong brothers didn't get hold of it)
when their wonderful flying machine took off at Kitty Hawk
into the kingdom of birds but the parliament of birds was
freaked out
by this man-made bird and fled to heaven

And then the famous Spirit of Saint Louis took off eastward and
flew across the Big Pond with Lindy at the controls in his leather
helmet and goggles hoping to sight the doves of peace but
he did not
Even though he circled Versailles

And then the famous Yankee Clipper took off in the opposite
direction and flew across the terrific Pacific but the pacific doves
were frighted by this strange amphibious bird and hid in the
orient sky

And then the famous Flying Fortress took off bristling with guns
and testosterone to make the world safe for peace and capitalism
but the birds of peace were nowhere to be found before or
after Hiroshima

And so then clever men built bigger and faster flying machines and
these great man-made birds with jet plumage flew higher than any
real birds and seemed about to fly into the sun and melt their wings
and like Icarus crash to earth

And the Wright brothers were long forgotten in the high-flying bombers that now began to visit their blessings on various Third Worlds all the while claiming they were searching for doves of peace

And they kept flying and flying until they flew right into the 21st century and then one fine day a Third World struck back and stormed the great planes and flew them straight into the beating heart of Skyscraper America where there were no aviaries and no parliaments of doves and in a blinding flash America became a part of the scorched earth of the world

And a wind of ashes blows across the land
And for one long moment in eternity
There is chaos and despair

And buried loves and voices
Cries and whispers
Fill the air
Everywhere

Andy Young

Circles of Lebanon

Please find a map attached of the attacks on Lebanon, July 12–22
—an email from a friend in Beirut to the author

purple dots show major cities,
white dots: small towns

each name's ringged in red:
one ring for 1–5 strikes,
two for 6–15

tidy circles inside a square
your country, Rasha,
a pocked gray shape
in my inbox

I search for unringed names
and find eight cities, no small towns

the circles cover and spread, a virus
under a microscope

three rings for 16–30
four rings around Baabda
more than 30 strikes
these last ten days

I zoom in to count again
yes: only eight cities, no small towns

Helba Tripoli Batroun Baalbeck
Hasbaiya Sannine el Marj my friend
there are too many to read to write
too many too many too many

Beirut's three circles radiate into the sea
as if the water were red, not black with oil

to the east and south: four
rings with no epicenter
          these must be the places
          I've seen on the news, grids
          of dust in satellite shots

within the thicker red
thin-fonted Ghobeiry, Haret Hreik,
Hadath, Hazmieh, Borj el Barajneh

they, too, stretch out to the sea
          the way we imagine sound
          from a drawn mouth
          or signals from antennae

they overlap with Beirut's rings

I wonder, again, where exactly
you live where
          in the rings you are

          I try to imagine them as halos
          of raindrops on a lake

Yater Marjaayoun
Hasbaiya Nabatiyeh

highways—gray lines—fissure across
the white spaces
                    is it the white space
                    people flee to?

you will not answer
for you have tired of words

I tap in a vacuum,
          notes of shock ricochet

E. Ethelbert Miller

Burial in the East (Entierro en el Este)

I could drop a nuclear bomb on any Lebanon in the world
and no one would care. A silence would sip tea or coffee in a cafe.
My son would play video games while my daughter talked
on the phone.
I could walk back into my house after murdering millions of people
and my wife
would only wonder if I was having an affair. Lately the legs of
oppression seduces me
everytime I see her. I was in the airport last week
and a man told me to remove my shoes. I did. I kept my wings on.
They are killing angels on the borders of Pakistan. Little girls
struggle to read on their
way to Mecca.There are civil wars in the world somewhere
but we don't want to call
them civil wars. When a bomb falls there is often nothing
left but dust and language. I
was once a slave before slavery was invented. John Brown
never met Pablo Neruda.

Gale Jackson

Brooklyn Baghdad Beirut Hiroshima

for Cintia

When the rain fall it don't fall on one man's
house.

June.

"Lebanon" Cintia writes
an eighth grade girl's dream assignment
"is the most beautiful country" called home
in our immigrant city where a nineteen year old
father neighbor crouches behind garbage cans and
shoots it out with the cops like they do
in the westerns

We live
never knowing when the day
will shatter

The groom
mourning the massacre
rained on his wedding
feast.

A car in the market
exploding
dust fire tongues
and a man running
baby in arms
infant face contorted
like walls collapsing
cry crushed
whimpering.

July.

Streets relinquish their hold
to sand in my dreams
but we wake to the beast flutter
of helicopter a child crying
and the sound particular
to this animal
of bombs exploding.

Could we have forgotten
ourselves?

The road out blocked skies aflame
bloody eye of moon
dear Nana daughter
of children who lived through and lost
so much in the world wars says
"I can't bring myself to like fireworks"
and another woman tries to trick
fear pretending the drum beat
leveling our town is a celebration
fourth of July in Brooklyn
as I watch a little tow head boy leap
with each burst
"ratatat-tat ratatat-tat"
in the home of the free
his small hands mock weapons his
tiny body a missile propelled further
from his mother intoxicated
and the crowds turning from
one spectacle of bombs bursting
to see the implosion.

That's my old woman
in the photograph on the front page
of the newspaper stunned bruised
but alive thank god I know her anywhere

her careful dress belying the rubble
that was our home Bint Jbail behind her
on the stretcher her hand
raised, familiar as my own
in a gesture of thanks
a manners among shards
on her lips
the unsung song's refrain
no more pictures of the dead
I beg you
for the challenge of the living
and the integrity of peace
and dignity.

August.

Oh my god
Oh dios mio
ave maria
inshallah

Hiroshima
and still?
Marking the day
of the dead
the day of never
again
with the blood
of farmers
and city dwellers
of sweethearts
and young men
with big guns
eye for eye
torn beyond vision.

But this is an old story
and we all know how the ancient conqueror

sow the dragon's teeth and reap a killing field

Here it must end to begin
beyond language borders crimes and sins
beyond the face of gods your telling or mine
you and I have one fate
the rain falling
an inundation that will drown us all
or an anointing.

Robert Bagg

Yeah

it's about Eyerak

Let's free their terrified
off-white eyes   a whole people
congealing   in a crazed
cracked shell   feeding and warming
their yellow   sucking
yolkmeister   armed
to his smile-proof teeth   he
has them covered   from inside
out   even though   they
surround him   the whole
crush through a vast desert
moves like a mass grave
still as warm   their deaths
a squeeze away   the meister's
oompahing heart bulging their brainpans

let's take him out   let's
cleanse   them   us   the works
let's go in   surgeons parting flesh
we squeeze   they burst   he
dazes up from a black hole
let's bury his protection
liberate his corpses   spirit
him away   into bulletproof
civilized   lawclothes   we've cut
to fit just him

Samuel Hazo

For Which It Stands

Crosswinds have slashed the flag
so that the thirteenth ribbon
dangles free or coils around
the flagpole like a stripe.
What's left
keeps fluttering in red-and-white
defiance.
Somehow the tattering
seems apropos.
The President
proclaims we'll be at war forever—
not war for peace, but war
upon war, though hopefully not here.
Believers in eternal re-election
hear his pitch and pay.
In Washington
God's lawyer warns we stand
at Armageddon, and we battle
for the Lord.
Elsewhere, California's
governor believes in California's
governor, and football bowls
are named for Mastercard, Pacific
Life, Con-Agra and Tostitos.
Out west a plan to gerrymander
Colorado (Texas-style) fails,
but barely,
Asked why no flag
is studded in his coat lapel
or decorates his aerial, a veteran
responds, "I wear my flag
on my heart—and I don't wear
my heart on my sleeve."

Today
for once we're spared the names
of occupying soldiers shot
or rocketed to fragments in Iraq.
Collateral damage?
Two boys,
their mother and both grandparents.
No names for them.
Just Arabs.

Sarah Browning

Sunday Morning, Spring

We eat and the world watches.

An angry flag whips the air,
the wind of a bomb

singing through the desert—
who wants to know the landing?

It is the singing we want,
the standing and the singing.

I am telling you—look. Do not
turn the page. Tear out

the bikini ad, burn it. Those women's
bodies might find their twins

floating in the light above the desert.

Hammurabi, the Exalted Prince Who Made Great the Name of Babylon, Has Words from the Other Side of Death for Donald Rumsfeld

I bite my tongue and try not to curse you
I bite my tongue and try not to wish upon you
          what you visited on me and mine

my voice that ordered laws
to be engraved for all to see and hear
orphans and widows

          no no do not place that curse upon him they say to me
          they say to Hammurabi the protecting King
          those who accompany me in the green dark of death
          that is not what we do in the green dark of death

my code
even slaves had rights
even women cast out by their husbands
adopted sons prostitutes patients
even the oxen in the fields
builders barbers sailors
they all had rights
even the oxen in the fields

my words that have survived four thousand years
invasions depredations despoilment plunder
Persians Mongols Ottomans Arabs British
the first written words
          of history
for all to know and see

Hammurabi shield of the land

that now lies
            broken shattered made dust
the many words of Mesopotamia

You could have stopped this
Rumsfeld Lord of the Looters
Lord of the Black Dawn

the statuettes of birds and goddesses
crushed by hammers sliced by knives
the scrolls painted by these hands
that surround me in the mother dark
gone all gone

only my words written in stone
still with me here on this other side

            not for cursing they say to me
            not what we do here they say

            in the life after the dark of life
            we teach they say to me
            we wait they say to me
            clothed in green gentleness
            the mothering dark

and yet and yet
Rumsfeld Rumsfeld
who did not defend the words and the widow
if I do not curse you, who will?

the tyrant who has fled or is dying dead?
the tyrant who broke my code?
the people of my earth who cannot speak
for fear of the new occupant of the throne?
the far people at your homeland
muzzled by ignorance and dread
who pray to you their protector?

I am Hammurabi
shepherd of the oppressed and the slaves
I am the good shadow spread over the city

Who else is there left to speak?
If any one steal the property of a temple he shall be put to
    death

If any one steal the minor son of another he shall
    be put to death

If any one break a hole into a house he shall be put to death

                    No no no they say to me
                    we do not believe in death
                    not an eye for an eye they say

If a fire break out in a house and he who comes to put it out
cast his eye upon the property of the owner of the house, he
shall be thrown into that self-same fire

He shall be thrown into that self-same fire

                    No no no they beg of me
                    not a tooth for a tooth they say

He shall read my inscriptions and stand before me

                    not a tooth for a tooth they say

may the years of your rule be in groaning
years of scarcity years of famine
darkness without light
the removal of your name and memory from the land

                    not his children they say to me
                    do not say it they say to me

may Nin-tu the sublime mistress of the lands
    the fruitful mother
deny you a son
give you no successor among men
the pouring out of your life
like water into the mouth of the desert

nothing lower than you
day turned into night

If not Hammurabi then who will speak?
Hammurabi the provider of food and drink
Who clothed the gravestones of Malkat with green

If I do not

may the damnation of Shamash overtake you
deprived of water among the living
and spirit below in the earth
day turned into night
thrown into that self-same fire
that fell upon the children and the books

If I do not curse the transgressor

I bite my tongue and try not to say these words
I bite my tongue and try not to say the words
that have lived for four thousand years
and are now smashed in the rubble
of the land that was once Babylon

If I do not curse you

my code and your code broken in the ruins
your glory and my glory gone gone all gone

If I do not curse you, who will dare?

Frank Reeve

war dead

they keep to themselves in the winter wind
that drives the living under ground
        leaving silence behind

in the cold oak forest bent-winged owls
harvest the terrified animals
        that feed in the night

at dawn women in black gather
the bones of the everlasting dead
        with earth-stained hands

Lisa Suhair Majaj

The Coffin Maker Speaks

At first it was shocking—orders flooding in
faster than I could meet. I worked
through the nights, tried to ignore
the sound of planes overhead,
reverberations shaking my bones,
acid fear, the jagged weeping
of those who came to plead my services.
I focused on the saw in my hands,
burn of blisters, sweet smell of sawdust;
hoped that fatigue would push aside
my labor's purpose.

Wood fell scarce as the pile of coffins grew.
I sent my oldest son to scavange more,
but there was scant passage on the bombed out roads.
And those who could made it through
brought food for the living, not planks for the dead.
So I economized, cut more carefully than ever,
reworked the extra scraps.
It helped that so many coffins were child-sized.

I built the boxes well, nailed them strong,
loaded them on the waiting trucks,
did my job but could do no more.
When they urged me to the gravesite—
that long grieving gash in earth
echoing the sky's torn warplane wound—
I turned away, busied myself with my tools.
Let others lay the shrouded forms in new-cut wood,
lower the lidded boxes one by one:
stilled row of toppled dominos,
long line of broken teeth.
Let those who can bear it read the Fatiha

over the crushed and broken dead.
If I am to go on making coffins,
let me sleep without knowledge.

But what sleep have we in this flattened city?
My neighbors hung white flags on their cars
as they fled. Now they lie still and cold,
waiting to occupy my boxes.
Tonight I'll pull the white sheet
from my window.
Better to save it for my shroud.

One day, insha'allah, I'll return
to woodwork for the living.
I'll build doors for every home in town,
smooth and strong and solid,
that will open quickly in times of danger,
let the desperate in for shelter.
I'll use oak, cherry, anything but pine.

For now, I do my work. Come to me
and I'll build you what you need.
Tell me the dimensions, the height or weight,
and I'll meet your specifications.
But keep the names and ages to yourself.
Already my dreams are jagged.
Let me not wake splintered from my sleep
crying for Fatima, Rafik, Soha, Hassan, Dalia,
or smoothing a newborn newdead infant's face.
Later I too will weep. But if you wish me
to house the homeless dead,
let me keep my nightmares nameless.

—South Lebanon, 2006

Margaret Gibson

Fuel

I am, said the voice in the oil spill of rainbow radiance,
the angel of El, from the deserts and gulfs of El.

I looked for a face, flesh and blood I might hold
accountable, a name. It saw right through me. *Uriel,*

Eliel, Emmanuel, Fuel, said the angel. *Fuel?* I replied,
and a human form stood before me, a merchant

who turned to measuring my life as if I were cloth,
judging length and price by the distance between his elbow

and the tip of his middle finger. The arm wore camouflage
the shade of sand and bone. *You do what suits me,*

Fuel smiled. He tossed the dead man's arm aside. *Grenade,*
he said. Arched his eyebrows, shrugged.

John Balaban

Ibn Fadhlan, the Arab Emissary, Encounters Vikings on the Volga River, 922 A.D.

The Rus, as they are called, camped above the river
trading furs from a log hall, axed out by slaves.
The men—tall as date palms, blonde, tattooed—
had set a pole out front carved with gods
to which they offer things to bless their trade.
This was all I saw of their piety or conscience.
Caliph, they are the dirtiest creatures of God.

Each morning when the men stir out of sleep
a slave girl brings a bronze ablution bowl
first to the chief who washes his face, then
rinses his mouth, spits, and blows his nose
into the bowl which she carries around until
each has washed in the same filthy water.

When their lord died, a huge *sahira dakhma*
(the witch who rules the slavegirls) set them wailing
as they packed his corpse in black earth and
his men built a death ship with a funeral pyre.
They call this witch "Angel of Death" *Malak al-Mawt.*
She picked a girl to go with the dead lord, then
invited the men to fornicate with the slavegirl
drugged and lost in a crazy song.

Then the girl was led to the ship
where the lord, his corpse now washed,
lay on the pyre wreathed in flowers and fruit.
Then the woman stabbed the girl
in her ribs as a man crept behind her
with a knotted rope, strangling her cries
until she fell dead and they laid her on the pyre.

Torching the ship, knocking away its blocks,
they shoved it blazing in the river, singing
their lord to a life of pleasures they imagine.
Soon his ship was ashes swirling on the currents.
O Caliph, through forested lands, west and north,
one finds only infidels with vile habits.
Some are Christian. Nothing will come of them.

Frank Reeve

The Blue Cat Writes to His Cousin in Baghdad

Anis al-Jalis, *sabah al khair!*
Heavy storm clouds from the East
brought the bad news: another ambush,
this month a thousand dead, a girl—
hope of the future—belly slit
by shrapnel, one-legged, blood-covered, blind—
does the army this morning roar in anger?
do citizens shake their fists in fear?

Sweet long-haired cousin, your dark brown eyes
bearing the burdens of Babylon
watch over the space between time past
and what becomes as every morning
your two great rivers wash the night down
and the sun rises red from the water.
Here we curl up in the flag and say nothing:
our public words make only lies.

I hear your voice in the twilight calm
arising from the man-high reeds
like Ishtar's magic above the river
when kings and princes fell in love
and old men stared and wagged their beards
and young men undid their belts. O Anis,
child of Shamash, king of heaven,
may you live forever. *Maasalaama, maasalaama.*

Grace Cavalieri

War Theater

They are not going quietly on stage.
But with a sighing, a whisper, a moan,
before they fall
against the white sheet of day. Now
the backdrop turns crimson, victims
of color and sweat.

In the theater of war the costumes are paper,
ripped and held together by pins. The intention
is obvious. A convention of the perishable!
When will the audience stop clapping and come forward?

The program says this is *The Age of Optimism*,
That a sharp consciousness of inquiry is required,
That a weak heart does not win wars,
That no illegal operations are performed,
That outside a green leaf still grows,
That the stage lights are a pure state of sun.

But the actors are hurt and I am afraid.
The stench inside is heavy with earth.
I break open the doors marked *no exit*.
So much light, I thought it was morning.

Ammiel Alcalay

I moved as free as light and as we sailed that strange
boat my dreams were fire like many voices walking forth
to awake the ruined labyrinth the motions of the crew
struggling until the stars spread from every tent I knew
that ship once made all things subject to its power as if
it drowned in remembrance and left the shades the only
living thing token flowers on the ground that night we
moved towards home a robe of glory beyond the sun
beyond the stars on the verge of formless space the grate
of brass the brazen rust the shadow in which friends return
like birds from the world's raging sea invested with the light
of language accents sounds a sense of actual things to weave
it was not art but some memorial like ice still clung to me
she was all I had her willing feet followed where I went
in the murmur of her dreams like the secret bird my hand
not a ghost's but warm with human blood these words had
fallen the secret of this world pierced as if the light was not
withdrawn for ever the past come again like wonder our
scattered tribes no longer blind cast off their memories
descending on still waters as whirlpools draw all wrecks
to their chasm to unfold to hear a strange and awful tale
the likeness of a shape a trace in gold imagined silver the
ages bear away those subtle nets which snare the living and
the dead of history as others know all its many names this
was ours the knowledge and the power justice a glance as
keen as lightning its shade a war that never failed to lick its
yellow light of wisdom to gaze on their spent and faded
luster woven beneath the veil like shelter in the desert

Elmaz Abinader

Where the Body Rests

Allah! Forgive our living and our dead, those of us who are present and those who are absent, our young and our old, our males and our females. O Allah! .... Allah is Great.

Our skin has turned to parchment
Our skin has turned to parchment
Our skin are the scrolls upon which
this history will be written

When your skin becomes phosphorous
speckled, yellow and scorched
Each cell is a star, constellations
flung upwards to create a new sky

When your skin is shredded
pounded to dust, you are not dead.
you are Instead ground into the earth
fertile and ready to plant

When your body detaches leaving
pieces of itself on the road
eyes are tiny pebbles the fist
a pine cone, corpuscles of Indian paintbrush

The deaths of innocents are not buried
or easily disposed of, no cloth can
wrap us tightly, no coffin an inpenetrable
shell. We are not dust but
the mark is on the earth, the vapors
are in the sky, the arteries of the heart
are the rivers and streams, our hair waterfalls.
We are clouds and boulders, brush and willow.
Our skin has turned to parchment

Our skin has turned to parchment
Our skin are the scrolls upon which
This history will be written

Etel Adnan

Palestine

As Arab men fall like
grapes from a vine
under late afternoon
summer's shine women
watch their bridal beds
crumble under bombs.
Separated on earth by
different pressures they
will meet again only in
a promised paradise.
They will not be the same.
Shadows will meet shadows.
The new Jerusalem will be
of no consolation for
the one they lost.

Melanie Kaye/Kantrowitz

Palestine in April 2003

Palestine: in April 2003: A hotel in Baghdad that housed journalists, bombarded by a US tank, killing three reporters.

Palestine: in April 2003: A town in Texas outside which an oil tank mysteriously exploded.

Palestine: in April 2003: A town in West Virginia, home of PFC Jessica Lynch, the rescued wounded soldier. Except she wasn't rescued, there were no guns, no guards, no danger; the hospital put her in the cleanest room, with the best bed, the one least likely to give bedsores, the Iraqi doctor explained. Then they notified the US Army so soldiers could come get her.

And finally: Palestine: in April 2003: A would-be nation, nothing new, only the time of year when Jews are bound to tell the story of our liberation and thus, like it or not, our story is bound to the story of the people our people oppress. And when at the end of our seder we say Next Year in Jerusalem hadn't we better smash open our hearts to lodge the frightened truth: that Jerusalem is also theirs; that peace and home are also their birthright; that those who called it a land without people for a people without land were simply wrong.

Reja-e Busailah

In the Shadow of the Holy Heights

for Haniya Suleiman Zarawneh, killed by the Israelis, at the age of 25, near Jerusalem, January 4, 1988

The sun came out that day from the depth of winter
like the rare orphan of good luck—
what else can the light of heaven be
on a day rising from the dead of winter?

And she had risen before the sun that day
and like her mother and grandmother before her
she washed by hand and wrung by hand
the linen for spouse and child;

and like mother and grandmother
she walked up the wooden ladder
with the pail onto the roof
into the shadow of the Holy Heights—
so clear was the sky
it almost recalled the sight and the scent of the sea down west.

Faithfully she hung her labors on the rope
article by article
that the good sun might dry them for her,
she clasped each with a wooden pin
as safeguard against the prankish wind—

it was no senseless nature that did it when she was done
just about to come down for other chores,
it was no fiendish fascist,
no obscene Nazi;
it was one of the Chosen
selected her heart for his anointed lead
so that limp went the spring in the covenant
which joined soul and limb—

and the good sun shines
and the sheets and the skirts and the nightgowns
and the small socks
and the outfit for the wooden doll
they toss in the wind
and smell like linen hand-washed and sun-dried
they swing lighthearted on the rope
waiting for mother to collect them.

Seema V. Atalla

Gift

One afternoon
you tried to give me Jerusalem

Knobbly onion domes
purple windows stained with God's tears
carrot juice, cobblestones
your girlhood ringlets, sunny laugh
the very gates of the Old City
so faithfully embroidered

It was impossible—too precious
the gift, too short the time
or so I thought then

You suffered, like Jerusalem
and left us

Now I think of your finger
the one that clutched a live wire
the day you nearly fell off the roof
the pinkie forever clenched, scarred
stunted
a lifeline that never healed.

Decades later, oceans away, I want to tell you:
I have it.
The gift you tried to give me, I've found it
it's been with me all along

Jerusalem like a blue bead embedded in my tongue
Jerusalem like a rock in the pit of my stomach
ring whose metal digs into my skin
ache under one rib, which never goes away

Jerusalem
the pain cross-stitched into my heart
with a needle that pierces both ways:
going in, and coming out.

James Scully

Donatello's Version

1

is unexpected:

the boy David
shamelessly naked,
one adorable leg
cocked at the knee

nonchalant
vulnerable
soft-bodied
a true killer

he wears his helmet
like a bonnet,
its pointy peak
garlanded with laurel leaves

2

the kid's a winner

little penis
big sword

standing astride
the craggy winged
head of the giant, Goliath

3

Goliath's head is peaceful,
his death like any death

is restful, untroubled
by desire or regret

4

David's skin glistens, obscurely
under a patina of melancholy

what's wrong with him

he should be dancing up and down
with joy

5

poor David
the good guy

victory is the worst thing
that could befall him

6

in the glass of his great victory,
through the loathsome mist
of world weariness

he sees himself
becoming *King* David

7

sees strings of victory
twining into distance
with strings of defeat

how he will conquer
and flee

how puff himself up
to hide

how he will dance around the sociopathic Saul

how marry, sire, beget
betrayals, adulteries,
murders, torture
prisoners raked
through the brick kiln

a weakness for poetry
will have him writing psalms
again and again—

for all he has won
by this great victory
is his own disaster:

his family, his kingdom, his people
tearing apart and apart

8

he will go through life
eating flesh by the fistful

choking on shadows

9

in the improbable blood
of his great victory

he sees all this
and is famished

Lisa Suhair Majaj

Fifty Years On / Stones in an Unfinished Wall

for Palestine

1
Fifty years on
I am trying to tell the story
of what was lost
before my birth

the story of what was there

before the stone house fell
          mortar blasted loose
          rocks carted away for new purposes, or smashed
          the land declared clean, empty

before the oranges bowed in grief
blossoms sifting to the ground like snow
quickly melting

before my father clamped his teeth
    hard
          on the pit of exile
slammed shut the door to his eyes

before tears turned to disbelief
disbelief to anguish
anguish to helplessness
helplessness to rage
rage to despair

before the cup was filled
raised forcibly to our lips

fifty years on
I am trying to tell the story
of what we are still losing

2
I am trying to find a home in history
but there is no more space in the books
for exiles

the arbiters of justice
have no time
for the dispossessed
without credentials

and what good are words
when there is no page
for the story?

3
the aftersong filters down
like memory
echo of ash

history erased the names
of four hundred eighteen villages
emptied, razed

but cactus still rims the perimeters
emblem of what will not stay hidden

In the Jaffa district alone:

Al-'Abbasiyya
Abu Kishk
Bayt Dajan
Biyar 'Adas

Fajja
Al-Haram
Ijlil al-Qibliyya
Ijlil al-Shamaliyya
al-Jammasin al-Gharbi
al-Jammasin al-Sharqi
Jarisha
Kafr 'Ana
al-Khayriyya
al-Mas'udiyya
al-Mirr
al-Muwaylih
Ranitya
al-Safiriyya
Salama
Saqiya
al-Sawalima
al-Shaykh Muwannis
Yazur

all that remains
a scattering of stones and rubble
across a forgotten landscape

fifty years on
the words push through

a splintered song
forced out one note
at a time

4
The immensity of loss
shrouds everything

in despair
we seek the particular

light angling gently
in single rays

> *the houses of Dayr Yasin*
> *were built of stone, strongly built*
> *with thick walls*
>
> *a girls' school   a boys' school   a bakery*
> *two guest-houses   a social club   a thrift fund*
> *three shops   four wells   two mosques*

a village of stone cutters
a village of teachers and shopkeepers

an ordinary village
with a peaceful reputation

until the massacre

> *carried out without discriminating*
> *among men and women*
> *children and old people*

in the aftermath
light remembers

light searches out the hidden places
fills every crevice

light peers through windows
slides across neatly swept doorsteps
finds the hiding places of the children

light slips into every place
where the villagers were killed
  the houses, the streets, the doorways
light traces the bloodstains

light glints off the trucks

that carried the men through the streets
like sheep before butchering

light pours into the wells
where they threw the bodies

light seeks out the places where sound
was silenced

light streams across stone
light stops at the quarry

5

near Qisraya, circa 1938
a fisherman leans forward,
flings his net
across a sea slightly stirred
by wind

to his left
land tumbles
rocky   blurred
to his right
sky is hemmed
by an unclear
horizon

(ten years
before the *Nakbeh* —

the future
already closing
down)

6
fifty years later
shock still hollows the throats
of those driven out

without water, we stumbled into the hills

a small child lay beside the road
sucking the breast of its dead mother

outside Lydda
soldiers ordered everyone
to throw all valuables onto a blanket

one young man refused

almost casually,
the soldier pulled up his rifle
shot the man

he fell, bleeding and dying
his bride screamed and cried

he fell to the earth
they fell in despair to the earth

the earth held them
the earth soaked up their cries

their cries sank into the soil
filtered into underground streams

fifty springs on
their voices still rise from the earth

fierce as the poppies
that cry from the hills each spring

in remembrance

7
some stories are told in passing
barely heard in the larger anguish

among those forced out
was a mother with two babies

one named Yasmine
and another
whose name no one remembers
her life so short
even its echo
is forgotten

the nameless child died on the march

it was a time of panic
no one could save a small girl

and so her face crumpled
lost beneath the weight of earth

I know only that she loved the moon
that lying ill on her mother's lap
she cried inconsolably
wanted to hold it in her hands

a child
she didn't know Palestine
would soon shine
          unreachable
     as the moon

8
the river floods its banks
littering the troubled landscape

we pick our way amid shards
heir to a generation
    that broke their teeth on the bread of exile
    that cracked their hearts on the stone of exile
    necks bent beneath iron keys to absent doors

their lamentations
an unhealed wound

I was forced to leave my village
but the village refused to abandon me
my blood is there
my soul is flying in the sky over the old streets

fifty years on

soul still seeks a sky

9
the walls were torn down long ago
homes demolished
rebuilding forbidden

but the stones remain

someone dug them from the soil
with bare hands
carried them across the fields

someone set the stones
in place on the terraced slope

someone planted trees,
dug wells

someone still waits in the fields all night
humming the old songs quietly

someone watches stars chip darkness
into dawn

someone remembers
how stone holds dew through the summer night

how stone
waits for the thirsty birds

The italicized sections of this poem are taken, in most cases verbatim, from historical and journalistic sources. The listing of destroyed villages and the passage beginning "All that remains" in section 3 is taken from Walid Khalidi's All That Remains: The Palestinian Villages Occupied and Depopulated by Israel in 1948 *(Washington D.C: Institute for Palestine Studies, 1992). The description of Deir Yassin in section 4 is taken from the Deir Yassin OnLine Information Center www.deiryassin.org). Section 5 refers to a photo in* All That Remains. *The description of refugees leaving Lydda in section 6 is taken from Father Audeh Rantisi's* Blessed are the Peacemakers: The History of a Palestinian Christian *(cited on www.alnakba.org/testimony/audeh.htm). The passage beginning "I was forced to leave my village" in section 8 is taken from a Reuters report by Nidal al-Mughrabi, April 14, 1998.*

Melanie Kaye/Kantrowitz

Jerusalem Shadow

[Excerpt]

for you were strangers in exile

I sit drinking tea on the balcony of the house you were raised in
where evenings your grandparents cousins sipped tea
told stories in Ladino   but you are named in Hebrew Haya
meaning *life*   the sun washes my skin
you talk of walks through East Jerusalem
of the lost backpack returned
intact   with a gift of fresh *pitot*
these things changed you   opened you
you fill my cup again
it's morning on the *Rechov Nisim Bekhar* in West Jerusalem
Jewish Jerusalem
I am your guest
you are yourself
not a mirror   not a statistic

this might be my home   but is not
I was born all over the planet   this time in Brooklyn
I came here looking for the seas to part
and truth to rise up
wet and obvious

I sit on the pink-grey stone by the Damascas Gate
eating hummous the sun is lavish direct   you
sit one step up in a black robe a white headdress
beside you a boy   *my brother* you tell me   later
after we catch each other's eyes   after we smile once
and again   until you pat the stone by you
motion for me to come sit   your name
is Ma'ha you want the English word for my sunglasses
for the digital watch you wear with your black robe
you say, *you like hummous?*

I nod smile speak neither English *yes*   nor Hebrew *ken*
though I'm sure you know *ken*   I don't know *yes* in Arabic
I think you know I'm a Jew
your watch shows 12:01
noon by the Damascas Gate in East Jerusalem
Arab Jerusalem   I am your guest
you are yourself
not a victim   not a symbol

I came here seeking a thread and see
a shadow or is it a woman
or two women shifting back and forth on the same spot
looking alike though at first
you wouldn't see it the hair skin
language almost comprehensible
salaam shalom

and which is the stranger
whose flesh was torn
who grabs whose sleeve
who eats dark bread and potatoes
whose teeth stain dark from the tea
whose tongue was formed abruptly in kitchens
in whispers   quick   quick

and which century do I mean
when does one woman become the other
when does the rooted one who belongs
transform into the one forced out
when does the one forced out and out and out
return to force out
and when does the other return
and how

here are some facts:

peace is not an absence
victims are not ennobled
home is the storm's eye unless
the stranger too is welcome

we were strangers in exile

5745–5746   1985

Dennis Brutus

Exile, exile
you are a bitter word
I eat you with my break
I drink you with my tea
you are the bitter word
that makes the world bitter to me

The stars look down
they see the world
they see a place
where I cannot be

Exile, exile
you are a bitter word
I eat you with my bread
I drink you with my tea
Exile, exile
you make the stars bitter to me

James Scully

Dadalab

1

the beginnings of dada
were not the beginnings
of an art
but of a disgust

so Tristan Tzara in 1922

dada came to be
the shrine of a urinal
—fountain of poverty—
signed into an art museum

a pig in an army uniform
floating overhead,
the Prussian archangel
swimming through air
kicking its little boots, grunting
"High from the Heavens I Come"

Hugo Ball nonsense syllables
dada babble
blowing up like body parts
shoulders of words hands arms legs
of words
fleeing the Great War

weird humor

scatting lines
in the sand
between art and pissy death

2

dada judo turns
newspapers, cripples, ticket stubs
into dada ads

not to disavow art, but
to shred its
illusory transcendence

to make visible the violence
of business as usual,
its chaos and hypocrisy

laughing like mad

dada was all for
vomiting itself
out of the Great War

3

Janco Dada Museum
the heart of Ein Hod
is also built upon
art thrown up by war

a not so great war

Ein Hod = Ayn Hawd
a village in 1949
the Jews drove the Arabs
out of

its haunting emptiness
evoked, then, biblical ruins—
here was a heavensent
construction site

to mystify the bounds
of art and life

to metamorphose
dada, the art of war,
into a bubbly art movement
where, in the Dadalab,
art concocts reality—

everything is possible,
objects like a refrigerator
or a table or picture
can go through walls,
a pot becomes an animation apparatus,
the imagination spreads its wings
and soars high

says the museum brochure

and in truth, in this
art that's a kind of anti-art
everything *is* possible

the Arabs who squat on a hill
a mile or so from home
live without electricity
without water, without a road,
without wings

imagine living without wings,
and yet they do

as animation apparatuses,

present absentees
like tables or pictures
that can go through walls

because the ends of dada
like its beginnings
are not the ends of an art
but of a disgust

troubling the ghosts of Ayn Hawd
whom museum walls go through

Seema V. Atalla

Holy Land

Head
bent in the heavy
halo of lamplight
stitch by tiny
stitch
how patiently
you occupied
the evening

Painstaking
such delicate detail
precise
the perfect petals
vines entwining
leaf by tiny
leaf

(Besieged by sudden
borders)

Settlements sewn
to the hills
bases secured
with double knots
checkpoints pinned
to the perforated
fabric

Calm
in the cornered crook
of a sofa's arm

Land spread flat
in that holy glare
altered
by invading needles
villages picked apart
old roads unraveling

Melia
counting the careful squares
within confining lines—
surrounded

The scarlet skeins
and veins of your hands
fill the grid
cross
by cross
with piercing
color

Richard Schaaf

In Hebron

1

The father is shaking
his fist at it
shouting at us:

Look at where my kids
used to play! Look at it!

Look at this barbed cage!

2

Before, it's where
the kids would play
soccer
tag
    in the freshly plowed
earth and dung

or mimic
the morning sparrows
        hopping, chirping
sowing laughter
among the olive groves

3

The mother is standing there
so silent silent
staring clear through us

She can't bear to look
at her kids
at the fear
there

looking back
at her

4

The father won't stop
shouting
at the world
to hear him

The kids won't ever ever
again
be kids

And the mother refuses
to give in
          rooted deep
in her anger and her land
staring clear through everything:

see what the Zionists have made of us!

Wade Fletcher

Unmovable

for Rachel Corrie

Little distinguishes bombs from bulldozers,
the latter, with its prescribed yellow and black with
iron blade, a favorite toy as a child,
my micro-scaled replica once so innocent,
now representing such a simple vehicle
of mass destruction; blade crushing skull, crushing
hope, flattening houses, bringing on tears,
pushing piles of rubble off, away, to be
replaced by settlements and barbed wire,
future reminders of where home once stood.
She stood there plainly, her body her
only weapon, at once a plea for peace
and a fierce demand, wielding her privilege
with defiance, staring down both life and death.

Kathy Engel

Harvesting Strawberries

In summer
my teenage daughters
hair waving freckles,
legs and arms swinging,
walk barefoot to the garden in our back yard,
pick greens,
wash them, make salad
or cook with olive oil and garlic
and we eat together
on the wooden table under the mimosa tree
beside hammocks and chimes,
then drive or walk three miles to plunge in the Atlantic.
On January 4, 2005
six Palestinian children ages eleven to seventeen
harvesting strawberries
were killed by Israeli military
paid, in part, with dollars we send in taxes
from our jobs.
A newspaper photo showed an almond eyed boy
carrying the body of his younger brother.
The children were harvesting strawberries.

Margaret Gibson

Moment

Just now, as I'm listening to the rain plink off the rim
of the down-spout,
she is walking toward the embassy,

the explosives hidden beneath her clothing,
swaddled against her belly,
warmed by her heat.

As I rifle through pages and pages of poems in Machado's
Times Alone
in search of the golden wind

that quickens words like *jasmine, lemon*, in Tuzla
a young girl watches
a man stumble to his knees

at the edge of a field, his hands tied behind him, and
already she hears
the clink of the shovel

that will uncover his bones, and those of the others,
two winters and one
harvest hence.

Listening and muttering, riffling and watching, I look up,
startled to hear
soaking into the stones at the edge

of the woods, *Cocoon! Cocoon!* the call of a dove,
so murmurous and clear
I could follow it gladly

into silence and green shade. *Not now*, I tell myself.
Not now. Ask first
what it is such silence mystifies.

Who it implicates, who protects. What it refuses,
what construes.

Samuel Hazo

Intifada

Singly at first, then doubly,
 then slowly by the tens or twenties,
 then steadily on...
 Interviewed
 about the deathcount in Ramallah,
 one sergeant said, "We'll kill
 them all, but we'll never
 forgive them for making us do it."
Later he aimed his Uzi at a boy
 armed with a stone and a slingshot,
One general claimed his soldiers
 fired only rubber-coated bullets.
When asked about the difference
 to the dead, he frowned and shouted,
 "Their leaders and parents use
 these children as human shield."
Despite the contradicting photographs,
 pundits and lobbyists concurred.
After all, who could deny
 that boys with all their lives
 ahead of them would happily
 seek execution, that mothers loved
 to see their sons in open
 coffins, that choosing a brave
 death instead of a lifelong one
 was an option for fools?
 No one
 would claim that occupation
 to the occupied resembled daily
 suffocation,
 No one would add
 that suffocation or the fear of it
 begot a courage born

of desperation.
No one compared it
to the fate of being locked
in darkness in a stalled elevator
underground.
Like someone buried
upright and alive, anyone
trapped there would stop at nothing.

Sarah Browning

In a City of Barricades, I Dream of Baghdad

Inauguration, 2005

A man walks into a wedding
and detonates—lace and sweet cakes.
Who imagined love was immune?
One body alone has chosen this future.
We choose to object, cardboard coffins
in our streets. But we've nothing
to draw the cameras, or even the cops.
We make love and weep. We cannot stop.

Khaled Mattawa

Terrorist

Reading night and the fire that lances the sky,
reading day and the arabesques of strewn corpses,
I become my brother's Siamese twin.
Rubbing the ashes of his bones unto my face
I become his blue screams at birth.
And despite what I've told myself,
what I've grown to believe,
despite my bunkered heart and fortified skin,
my thick bile and phlegm,
I am bled white by an appalling battle.
I have cleansed my body with the soap of his fat,
stuffed my pillows with his shorn hair,
I made dice of his molars.
Everything, and my contradictions above all, bring us closer.
Will I walk on four now to recall what I thought was human?
Will I climb the tree shedding skin whispering the apple's secret?
What poisons will house themselves in my gills?
Will I be a victim again? And again a murderer?
I split in two and two more, and I fill a room
like yeast growing unto all the selves I've known.
Yet everything leads me back, unified
and cellular, to the womb we shared.
Reading thunder made in philosophers' salons,
reading lightning that severs the sun's rays,
everything brings us closer.
My silences spill an ooze that fastens me to him.
My cowardices hook us into one destiny.
See how short my arms are.
Take a look into my blind eyes.
Every breath I inhale is the cold wind
that makes us embrace like statues of eternal lovers.
In every exhale there's a wisp of silver
smoke from the warm clay that binds us.
Reading night, reading day,
I twin myself to my brother.

Kathryn Levy

Reports
[Excerpt]

In the place in the woods
where the shooting continues
a child reaches
her arm past an arm
and begs again—to
anyone—as the
shooting continues
a blind man locks
his body in a closet
but he still can hear
a woman bends over
her sewing machine
the shots the needle
pounding still pounding
a little boy clutches
rage in his fist he
holds it for decades
as a building tumbles
an explosion fails
to murder the rage so
he tries it again
the shooting continues
in anthems and speeches:
They have sacrificed
their right to exist
the little boy points
his gun at the sky and
the trees those leaves
the birds who keep flying
refusing to care that
the shooting continues—they
have to be taught
he pokes two fingers

into two eyes: I *can't*
see anymore—so I have to hang
onto this gun—but only until
he gets what he needs the pounding
the shooting continues

E. Ethelbert Miller

There are Oceans Left to Kill

Now they are shooting holes in all the holy leaders. But we don't know who they are. We are trapped between Iraq and a hard place. A burial ground, a land of insurgents and veils. Who is shooting whom? Men die and women die and children die and yesterday someone dropped a dead body from a car and pulled out a gun and shot the body again and again and it didn't matter if it was someone who was Shiite, Sunni or Syrian. The blood all flows together and lately what was a stream is now a river. There are oceans left to kill. There is blood on the windowsill and blood on the floor. There is blood knocking on the door and blood dancing barefoot in the road. There is blood praying at the mosque and blood calling people to prayer. There is blood saluting the living and blood burying the dead. There is blood in Baghdad and blood singing in Babylon. There is blood on a face and blood on a hand. There is blood without a head and blood on a knife. There is blood on me and there's blood on you. There's blood on the flag and blood on the books. They are shooting holes into air and into bones and flesh. They are shooting into dreams and shooting out nightmares. They are shooting soldiers and they are shooting fools. They are shooting into schools and shooting out wombs. They are shooting mothers and cousins, grandfathers and aunts. They are shooting uncles and brothers, sons and lovers. They are shooting daughters and sisters and shooting each other. There is no death left. There are no trees. There is no wind. There is no breeze. There is just a hole the size of life. A hole the size of death. There is only one coffin left. Now who will stand in line to wait to die? Who will wait to be shot? Who will wait to kill? Who will call the doctor? Who will pay the price? Who will make the sacrifice?

Whom should we forgive? What sinner will confess? Which God made this mistake? What night now finds its end? What day is this that breaks? What more can we endure? What bird no longer flies? What man no longer loves? What silent heart must learn the song of peace again? And sing again, and dream again, and come again.

Suheir Hammad

break

(nyc)

the humidity condenses breath

bodies stick and stones gather in a lower back

gray thick moving slow and alone

i am looking for my body

for my form in the foreign
in translation
what am i trying

to say i sit in this body dream
in this body expel
in this body inherit
in this body

here is the poem

i left a long time ago
remember stubble remember unwanted remember touch

i can't remember where i left my body

poem needs form lungs need
air memory needs loss i need
to translate my body because it is profane

what had happened was
i wrote myself out of damage

this is the body of words and spaces
i have found to re-construct

(deheisha)

my home
girl is there now the air is thick
people don't breathe well hold their
tongues against cursing all of existence
all that would carry on living during this

she wakes to news just the beginning
the same story the one which leaves bodies
behind as tokens of nothing

one family
roasting corn
now all husks
silk
spraying
wind

my home girl's body
would be called white be claimed jewish
is mother and loved by a man who sits in a bay
by telephone and radio and reaches for his lover's body
and finds only formless

she is witness and rage
i pray her body save her
come back with her offer lover a home
daughter a beginning and all of us testimony

the people there tell her they will survive this

if a body can carry through you follow

(beirut)

a green body obsessed white possessed
by all male religion sword sniper garnishes silicone radishes
video radiology vixens eastern european prostitution manic
depression olive oil sweat camps resorts hair gel all that is life
all that is death

the roads and bridges been hit
the airport been hit

where is a body to go

we lived there once my parents sisters and me
i left my skin there still boiling

(tel aviv)

write your own damn poem
build a grammar with something other than bones

(gaza)

a woman's hand cups bloodied sand bits scalp ooze
to the camera and says this is my family

(khan younis)

yammaaaaaaaaa
yammaaaaa

(nyc)

i am waiting for a break
in weather

i am not yet broken
enough to forget
desire but i wish i would

my parents worry i will never marry
i cannot comfort them

(houston)

a family says this is the summer of sacrifice
no vacation no new car no addition to the study
but pedicures and hair relaxing and shape-ups and gyms
mandatory a body must keep up must be presentable

a husband says i wake up and sleep and wake up
and all i think about is gas prices

(bombay)

bomb bay bomb bay bomb bay bomb bay

(exactly brooklyn)

my niece sleeps light
my sister feeds her her body
my clan holds one breath

(new orleans)

there is no wading in this water
a body can be polluted inside and out

(baghdad)

the children watch from bodies roasting by roadsides
they fall in love with the soldiers killing them
they see soldiers are bodies with orders
they wish for something to follow

a star an idea called hope sick as it sounds

(here)

is my body

is my body
an offering to give or to receive

wait for storm
know that even this is not it
that when it comes
break will be fire baptism
and in the ashes there
is my body

James Scully

Boxcars
[Excerpts]

17
look, what should have been
light is darkness

the lessons of the Holocaust
learned by rote
practiced over and over in the mirror
shatter their own image

soldiers of the Holocaust
cossack shadows rampage
across and across
the Holyland they dreamed
driving two-legged beasts
to extinction

18
in this dream, your dream,
we exist as present *absentees*
insects
          in perennial rubble
under a heaven of unforgiving genesis

whatever tells of us
who used to be human
is razed, obliterated, walled-up
          crushed
by bulldozers bigger than a house

19
your dream is a nightmare
because we are in it

we crowd streets between curfews your tank clanks through
slowly
sprays us with DDT

as though we're another species

we could be another species

we are born in boxcars,
the bad faith of boxcars,
the *carte blanche* of boxcars,
bundled under munitions
side by side
with dug up naked bones

our fathers mothers grandparents
uncles aunts, kids old as
stones, as dirt, as names, oranges, hearts
older than histories
are heaved up into them
            as wanderers
in battered trunks called the *demographic problem*

as who on earth isn't
a demographic problem
the more we are, the less we matter

look at us
we carry no weight
we miscarry
your missiles in the marketplace
we who have no missiles

with us, now, the ghosted boxcars of the Holocaust careen
            so screamingly light
like a bad joke gone really bad
they threaten to fly, fly, dragged
                                    off the rails, to crash
this only life on earth we are passing through

because when our species ends
yours does too

Jack Hirschman

Never Again

They were gassed, burned by the millions
simply because they existed.
Those who survived said: Never again!
They were asked to come to Hanoi
and continue the socialist revolution.
They responded: Never again!

We will never again trust any government.
We will make our home in Palestine,
defeat the Arabs there, scatter them or
let them live as ragged shadows
in the camps of our occupation.
We will live in and on the capital of America,

as Israel, by name, as the Jewish nation,
and never again be holocausted for
the crime of simply being.
But even as Israel grew and prospered,
those whom it displaced and arrested
were whispering: Never again!

Poor and landless, they built their resistance
and fought and lost again and again
to Zionism's army of American weapons.
The language of socialism, of the friendship
and harmony of peoples of different cultures
died of attrition in the Middle East, from

money. Deals. Dunny meals. Doomy mules.
Dummy moles. Mummy doles. The Star
of David unfurled over the land,
but the real Davids were in the streets
throwing stones at the Goliath.

O philistine irony and reversal of the Hebrew.

They who are the poorest and stateless,
who've turned their hatred of submission
to slavery into martyr brigades of suicided
Human weapons, and called their brethren
to join their attack upon the ferocious colony
of the United States of Exploitation;

they, the poorest and homeless, in whom
the only solution still breathes, the only
solution that isn't genocide or fratricide
or a final solution itself, where hand-clasp
and words can still mutually open the gates
to the language of the future socialism

of New Israel and New Palestine,
is where Never again!
will be the united cry
of both, aimed
at the land of the fraud
and the home of the greed.

Amiri Baraka

Enemy of Civilization

The Palestinians
call you "Enemy
Of the Sun," from a bunker
Barely able to see
The sky. But I
Here in the automatic
Dungeon of the DeAtop his slice of
Gold slobbering Evil
See what I see, &
It is not just The
Sun, the demon has
Declared teeth & claw
War, blood libel
No survival, They
It Them He from the
Loud canon of
Ignorant violence
Detest the idea of
Humanity. He It They
Them, call for the
Non-beginning the
Savage unbeing of
Anything that sees,
Hears, feels, is touched,
Can smell, anything that
Sings, anything, one, body,
Wants to create, not
Destroy or obliterate.
He It Them They have
Ruled history illegal
& the future a nutty
vision, the root of
all division, these

guys, dolls, gogs
Magogs, them heels
& charlatans, them
Heathens & beasts
& monsters & haints
those preposterous liars
truth deniers, Imbeciles
cannibals, omnivorous
criminals, dem wealthy
tramps, colossal
flesh eating ants,
them uncle and missile
Sams, them humiliated
losers in N Korea &
Viet Nam, has declared
Civilization treason
along with thought,
friendship & reason.
They, it them have
Said civilization &
Its provocateurs
Have got to be
Killed dead.
& further, said them
they it, beast, 666
proclaim those who
want to be human
insane.
NO, not just
Enemies of The Sun
But enemies of life
& the world, enemies
of humanity, & of
Civilization itself.
These are Amoebas
Of the 21st century,
One celled poisonous
Organisms, aspiring

To become hyperbotulistic
Viruses of disease
Ridden Capitalism
Smears of epidemic
Racism. Gods
Of the bottom of
The toilet bowl.
The Devil was old
Fashioned they mumble
We ain't humble
The Devil was a
Do-Gooder &
Everybody know
Anything near good
is deadly. That
Is what the Enemies
Of Civilization
Say (when they ain't
Lying)

Suheir Hammad

break (clustered)

all holy history banned
unwritten books predicted the past
projected future but my head
unwraps around what appears
limitless man's creative violence

whose son will it be
which male child will perish
a new day

our boys' deaths galvanize
we cherish corpses

we mourn women complicated
bitches get beat daily

profits made
prophets ignored

worn tooth enamel salted lemon childhoods

all colors run
none of us solid

don't look for shadow
behind me i carry it within

i live cycles of light and darkness
rhythm is half silence
i see now
i never was one
and not the other
sickness health tender violence

i think now i never was
pure before form
i was storm blind
ignorant still am

humanity contracted itself
blind malignant i
never was pure

girls spoiled before ripened
language can't math me
i experience exponentially
everything is
everything

one woman loses 15 maybe 20 members of her family
one woman loses 6
one woman loses her head
one woman searches rubble
one woman feeds on trash
one woman shoots her face
one woman shoots her husband
one woman straps herself
one woman gives birth to a baby
one woman gives birth to borders
one woman no longer believes love will find her
one woman never did

where do refugee hearts go
broken dissed placed
where they're not from
don't want to be
missed faced with absence

we mourn each one
or we mean nothing at all

my spine curves spiral

precipice running to and running
from humans beings

cluster bombs left behind
de-facto land mines

a smoldering grief

harvest contaminated tobacco
harvest bombs
harvest baby teeth
harvest palms
smoke
harvest witness
smoke
salvation
smoke
resolutions
smoke
redemption
smoke

breathe

do not fear what has blown up
if you must fear
the un-exploded

Sonia Sanchez

Peace

a poem for Maxine Greene

1. Peace. What is it?
   Is it an animal A bird? A plane?
   A mineral? A color? A drumbeat?
   (doowop doowop doo doo dee doo doo dee)

2. Is it a verb? A noun? An adjective?
   A prophet with no pockets?
   Circling our paragraphed lives?
   (dwoodop bopbop dwowaaa doo bop bop doo bop bop bop)

3. DuBois said: The cause of war
   is the preparation of war
   DuBois said: The cause of war
   is the preparation of war.
   I say the cause of peace
   must be the preparation of peace.
   I say the cause of peace
   must be the preparation of peace.
   (Blaablablabaaaa blue blueeblay blueeblay)

4. Shall I prepare a table of peace
   before you in the presence of mine enemies?
   Shall I prepare a table of peace
   will you know how to eat at this table?
   (skee dee dee dah dah doo dah bop dah bop bop dah boo)

5. Where are the forks of peace?
   Where are the knives of peace?
   Where are the spoons of peace?
   Where are the eyes of peace?
   Where are the hands of peace?

Where are the tongues of peace?
Where are the children of peace?
(Peace, Peace, ting ting tee tee peeeeace ting ting tee)

6. Is peace an action? A way of life?
Is it a tension in our earth body?
Is peace you and I seeing beyond
bombs and babies roasting on a country road?
(bop bop bop bop bop bop bop bop
bopooooooouеeeeeee)

7. Peace must not be still we have to
take it on the road, marching against
pentagon doors lurking in obscenity.
Peace must not find us on our knees
while a country holds hostage
the hearts and penises of the workers.
(bleep bleep bleep blueee bleep bleep blueee doo da boom
doo da boom)

8. Can you say peace? Can you resurrect peace?
Can you house the language of peace?
Can you write a sermon of peace?
Can you populate the chords of peace?
(dee dee dadum peace la la la la dum peace)

9. A long time ago someone said: I think therefore I am
A long time ago someone said: I think therefore I am
Now we say preemptive strikes therefore we are
Now we say preemptive strikes therefore we are.
(boom boom boom ay ay ay ay ay boom ay boom ay ayaay)

10. Can you rise up at the sound of peace?
Can you make peace lighter than air?
Can you make peace sing like butterflies?
Until peace becomes the noise of the planet
Until peace becomes the noise of the planet
(PeaceeEeeeeEeeeeEeeeEeeeeEeeEeeEeeeEE)

11. I know as MLK knew that the universe
is curved ultimately toward justice and peace.
I know as MLK knew that the universe
is curved ultimately toward justice and peace.
for "war is the sanction of failure"
for "war is the sanction of failure"
(dobam doom-doooobam dooooood doooom)

12. Martin said a riot is the language of the unheard
and I say a terrorist's bomb is the language of the unheard
how to make the unheard heard?
without blowing themselves and the world up?
how to make the unheard heard?
without blowing themselves and the world up?
(BOOOM BOOM BOOM BOOOMM BOOOOMMM)

13. Mos Def said: Speech is my hammer
bang my world into shape
now let it fall.
I say peace is my hammer
bang my world into peace
and let it fall on the eyes of children.
(frere Jacques dooodoodoo frere Jacques dooooo doooo
dormez-vous vous vous vous ding dong ding ding dong ding)

14. Where are the forks of peace?
Where are the knives of peace?
Where are the spoons of peace?
Where are the eyes of peace?
Where are the hands of peace?
Where are the tongues of peace?
Where are the children of peace?

15. Where are you—you—youuuuuuu (click)
where are you you you you youuuu (click)
you you where are you you
where you where are youuu (click)
click—click—you—youuu (click)

Andy Young

Mama Condi

What we're seeing here is, in a sense, the growing, the birth pangs of a new Middle East....

—Condoleezza Rice

who
will be yr
breathing coach
who will be yr daddy
when you squat & pant,
grunt & open
when yr skin
splits to make
way for bunk-
er bust- ers, las-
er guid- ed miss-
iles, for cluster
bombs, phosphor,
smoke & shrapnel,
char & cin- ders, baby
bomblets baby Con-
di you
can call it ME
for short Mama
Rice Ma
ma Condi birthing
the new Middle East, its
eyes blasted out its
tiny heart blown open

break (word)

yo thunder gun clap
flash flood warning

cumin kizbara a kiss bara
herb quartz strung key feather
door internet iced letters coffee clove guinness beats
beats beats july heat miriam medicine
what you become not just on paper
rasha kabab-ji wein wein wein wein il millaiyeen
beautiful bosom in love beirut

corner the corniche
stop lean against
a railing wave foreigners goodbye
turn and walk into a bomb

we no longer know language

a-sunder sun dare
ash judge warring

ribs borders razors geneva guava evacuate demonstrate
against blinding
emperor's mission religion

cain and able
the first civil war still raging

humiliate a people distract the rest

trademark star brand dreams
seeds water new world
old words this ain't living

words are against us
there is a math only subtracts

W.S. Merwin

Ash

The church in the forest
was built of wood

the faithful carved their names by the doors
same names as ours

soldiers burned it down

the next church where the first had stood
was built, of wood

with charcoal floors
names were written in black by the doors
same names as ours

soldiers hurried it down

we have a church where the others stood
it's made of ash

no roof no doors
nothing on earth says it's ours

Seema V. Atalla

Cold Comfort

The lost places are easy to list:

My grandmother's Haifa
where she wore her hair in waist-long braids,
gathered with her neighbors by the seaside to chat,
and ate the tiny, crisp fish she loved, fried to perfection.

My father's Nazareth
where he carried grain to the mill for his mother,
and listened to the blind man who sat outside the church
playing hymns on his flute.

My grandmother's Jerusalem
where she planted banks of fragrant lavender,
taught kindergarten,
and rolled grape leaves for dinner, leaf by leaf.

My mother's Ramallah
cool green peaceful place
where she and her sisters learned algebra and embroidery
among the sighing pines and rosy stone homes.

Those places are unrecognizable now
disfigured
by misery
riddled with desperation
choked with the nitty gritty grime of actuality.

Simpler to turn back to the long-cherished images.
The lost places seem quaint now,
perhaps a little faded…
we revisit them
the way we touch an old injury,

fingering the scar
over and over
finding comfort
in pressing the place
where it hurts.

Martín Espada

The God of the Weather-Beaten Face

for Camilo Mejía, conscientious objector

The gods gathered:
the crusader god took off his helmet,
the desert warrior god stood his shield in the corner,
the sword-maker god sat between them sharpening blades,
the bombardier god spread his maps on the table,
the god who collects infidel heads traded trophies
with the god who collects heathen scalps,
the god of gold opened his handkerchief
for the god of oil to wipe his dripping chin,
the god who punishes sin with boils scratched his boils
and called the meeting to order.

And the gods said: *War.*

Sergeant Mejía heard the prisoner moan under the hood
as the guards shoved him into a steel closet, then pounded
with a sledgehammer on the door until the moaning stopped;
heard machine gun fire slicing heads from necks
with a roar that would be the envy of swords;
heard a soldier sobbing in the toilet for the headless boy
who would open his eyes every time the soldier closed his own.

Sometimes a song drifts up
through the moaning and sledgehammers,
machineguns and sobbing.
Sometimes a voice floats above pandemonium
the way a seagull floats over burning ships.
Sergeant Mejía heard his father's song,
the peasant mass of Nicaragua:
Vos sos el Dios de los pobres,
el Dios humano y sencillo,
el Dios que suda en la calle,
el Dios de rostro curtido.

You are the God of the poor,
the human and simple God,
the God who sweats in the street,
the God of the weather-beaten face.

Iraq was crowded with the faces of this God.
They watched as Sergeant Mejía said *no* to the other gods,
miniscule word, a pebble, a grain of rice,
but the word flipped the table at the war council,
where the bombardier god had just dealt
the last hand to the god of oil,
and cards with dates of birth and death,
like tiny tombstones, fluttered away.
Sergeant no more, Camilo Mejía walked to jail.
Commanders fed the word *coward*
to the sniffing microphones of reporters
who repeated obediently: *coward*.

The cell crowded with faces too, unseen travelers
wandering in from a century of jails:
union organizer, hunger striker, freedom rider,
street corner agitator, conscientious objector.

The God of the weather-beaten face,
dressed as an inmate steering a mop,
smuggled in the key one day, and Camilo Mejía
walked with him through epiphany's gate.

Rashidah Ismaili

Yesterday, Today and Next Tomorrow
[Excerpts]

She said:

I am waiting for Ahmed.
Yesterday a letter came.
Yesterday a man came.
Yesterday a car came.
Yesterday, a letter, a man and car.
came and left with Ahmed.

He said to me, "Do not fear, my wife.
I shall just be a little while. Do not fear.
Go, do your work. Do not fear."
Last night, he said this to me.

I have waited.
I have tried not to fear.
I have not answered
when the telephone rang.
After the first call and second,
I refused to answer them.

I am waiting for Ahmed.
He was supposed to come home.
Yesterday, a fortnight, a year ago,
he was to come back, come home.

I have waited on cold benches
in long halls. Long halls with
bright lights, where rows and rows
of women who look like me—wait.

We wait day after day
for Omar, Ousmane, Ali, Jaafar!

Ahmed, I am waiting for Ahmed.
He said he would come home
when telex returned his identity,
when his status was confirmed...

..."Ahmed! Ahmed! Ahmed!"

I have called you three times.
I have sat with the others,
with all the waiting women
calling, calling your name.
I have said The Names
in all the corners and crevices
of this house you slept in, once...

Today, the hands that once
clasped a pen, fingers that once
lost themselves in my hair
are swollen and cannot close.
Today eyes that once held me
in the dark orbs of your heart
stared vacant and water

ran along a scar...

Frank Reeve

Country Life in Wartime

What can I do with the scraps of my life,
the peels and old papers dropped behind,
the unfossilizable past?

In the pasture small animal bones fill cracks
in the ledge, skulls lurk half-hidden like rocks—
(imagine instead their skins cast

not like snakes' but in shining bronze
or light-catching marble like David's loins
luring new lovers each day).

What a vision it was—the April full moon,
the free-loving Easter air, the upturn
of the year burling away—

when the rumble of war rolled it flat like a still
photo, fear unfurled on the hills,
and the old dog whined to come in.

The clock in the hall counts my long days;
midnight chimes its twelve like a knell,
each stroke a farewell to a friend

who died while the world and time were green.
The dead write no letters, go half-mourned;
a few were kind to the end.

Here the living hurry along
pursued by death, hoping that soon
death, too, will be banned

like disease, replaced by conforming desires
and the re-annealed rings of small failures,
golden on each hand.

See the beautiful immortals,
the once-young gods a-making love
in fields of asphodel.

Watch the dumb, blind, blue earth
turn brown and shrink like a pickled head
without a story to tell.

"Not us! Not us!" the leftovers cry.
No life, I see, without eyes. *Nada.*
Nobody here since you died.

Richard Schaaf

In Mosul

Washington Post, May 4, 2005

Now this full-bleed
front-page photo
released by the U.S. Army
courtesy of Getty

This soldier
in battle fatigues
on his knees
in the sand
in Mosul

cradling the child
the body of the child
in Mosul

He appears to
whisper something
in the child's ear

but what on earth
can he say

Grace Cavalieri

Fateema

She didn't know her thirst for song would
lead her to water,
telling stories to all
who would gather to hear.

The people came alive as they listened,
bringing her
vats, then jugs, and then cups of cool drink.

She wanted to write
legends on paper, words
that would not perish in flame.

All her life she'd walked the ridge of the village
sinking her feet
to the softness of dust,
a griot with vision, a truth in ink,
which did not soil history's page.

Now, in the rubble,
she'd open her heart and pass
back to the time
before she was five,
to the past where she sat on the lap of her mother
to hold onto her apron before it was gone.

Her mother said,
You will be a teller of stories
a writer of names.
When you lose everything to the stealer of pens,
remember this moment, the feel of my cloth.

She did not know that war
would dry the well,

or that no one left
could ease the cracked earth.

Yet because legends
living in the heart will not die,
even in a land
vanished of water,
she would draw from her bleeding dreams
to drink all the things she needed to say.

Sam Hamill

Eyes Wide Open

The little olive-skinned girl
        peered up at me
from the photograph

with her eyes wide open,

deep brown beautiful eyes
        that bore silent witness
to a grief as old as the ages.

She was young,
        and very beautiful, as only
the young can be,
        but within such beauty
as bears calamity silently:

because it has run out of tears.

I closed the magazine and went
        outside to the wood pile
and split a couple of logs, thinking,
        "Her fire is likely
an open fire tonight,
        bright flames licking
and waving

like rising pennants in the breeze."

When I was a boy,
        I heard about the bloodshed
in Korea, about the Red Army

perched at our threshold,
and the bombs
that would annihilate our world

forever.

I got under my desk with the rest of the foolish world.

In Okinawa, I wore the uniform
and carried the weapon
until my eyes began to open,
until I choked
on Marine Corps pride,
until I came to realize
just how willfully I had been blind.

How much grief is a life?
And what can be done unless
we stand among the missing, among the murdered,
the orphaned,
our own armed children, and bear witness

with our eyes wide open?

When I was a child, frightened of the night
and crying in my bed,
my father told me a poem or sang,

"Empty saddles in the o-l-d corral,
where do they r-i-d-e tonight."

Homer thought the dead arrived
into a field of asphodels.
"Musashino," near Tokyo, means
"Musashi's Plain,"
the warrior's way washed in blood.

The war-songs are sung
    to the same old marching measures—
oh, how we love to honor the dead.

A world without war? Who but a child or a fool
could imagine such a thing?

Corporate leaders go to school
    on Sun Tzu's *Art of War.*
"We all deplore it," the President says,
    issuing bombing orders,
"but God is on our side."

Which blood is Christian,
which Muslim, Jew or Hindu?

The beautiful girl with the beautiful sad eyes
    watches, but
has not spoken. What can she

possibly say?
    She carries the burden of finding
another way.

In her eyes, the ruins, the fear,
the shoes that can't be filled, hands
that will never stroke her hair.

But listen. And you will hear her small, soft, plaintive voice
—it's already there within you—

a heartbeat, a whisper,
a promise broken—
if only you listen

with your eyes wide open.

Grace Cavalieri

The Wall

The child stands weeping.
She holds uncooked rice in one hand waiting
to eat. She idealizes into a picture
for American Television
until the dial turns her away from our sight.

Teachers and writers hide behind walls,
their safety from pain, more important than
papers and books. The
sirens sound. The child embraces the wall, presses
her lips against stone.

A dog outside howls its
mortality. And that is all she hears before
the vision comes to mind of a mother
she once knew.

There are no clearly marked graves
for memory. Have faith, her grandmother told her.
Someone will come for us. Have faith. Words are
crashing trains in her mind.

The Book of Koran
lies open, naked, and torn in a broken house.
She huddles. The child cannot speak, and has
forgotten how language sounds. Should she run?
No roof is overhead to hold the
rain or falling fragments from her.

Can she run across the open courtyard?
Someone may be there. Her dog? Where?
Grandmother? Where? Rubble flies.
That was while she stood there clutching her rice
in the origin of silence.

Hayan Charara

Lucy

The phone call, from my wife.
"She's hungry, she's pregnant,
someone kicked her in the stomach—
we have to." I said yes,
but the reply I kept to myself was
We don't have to do a goddamn thing.
A dog. I'm talking about a dog
I would have otherwise left
to starve. Now, though, five years
after the fact, I love this animal
more than I can most people.
Except, none of this matters.
It's context to something else,
a boy, six years old, who twice
each day fed a dog, and five cats,
every single one he named
after ours, the rescue, Lucy.
The boy, my brother, born
in Henry Ford's hometown,
but who lives now in Bint Jbeil,
which the Greeks called Byblos,
and they tried but failed
to subdue it, same as the Egyptians,
Hittites, Assyrians, Babylonians,
Alexander the Great, Romans,
Arabs, Crusaders, Turks,
the Brits, the French, the Israelis.
There, my father built a house
with money earned in Detroit—
as a grocer, with social security.
Also there, the first alphabet
was created, the first law school
built, the first miracle of Jesus—
water, wine.

On the first day the bombs fall,
they flee, and the boy asks
to go back for Lucy, the dog.
As for the cats, "No.
They take care of themselves."
One week into it, he wonders,
who feeds them, who fills the water bowls.
Maybe the neighbors,
the mother thinks out loud.
The father is indignant—
"What neighbors?"
The mother is stunned—
"What do you mean, what?"
After a month, everyone forgets
or just stops talking about the animals.
Here, on the other side, we can't help
but shake our heads so to say,
Don't think about them.
During the ceasefire
my father drives south,
a thirty-minute trip
that lasts six hours—
wreckage upon wreckage
piled on the roads, on what
is left of the roads.
The landscape entirely gray,
so catastrophic he asks
a passer-by how far
to Bint Jbeil and is told
"You're in it."

They found three of the cats,
all perforated, one headless.
The dog was near the carport,
where it hid during lightning storms,
its torso splayed in half,

like meat on a slab;
its entrails eaten
by other dogs that also
scavenged on human corpses
littering the streets.
Look. They're animals.
Which is to say, there are also people.
And I haven't even begun telling you
What was done to them.

Kathy Engel

Warning

A small black bird
lay on its side
dead on the brick steps
claws in the air
long beak pointing east
neck soft.

I didn't hear killing
or dying
only the dog squealing to get to it.

With two shovels I scooped the bird,
not as large as my hand,
flip flopped it
to keep from touching or inhaling
even one floating piece of feather.

A current—death
moved from the lump of bird
through the shovel
to my hand and into my chest.
I expected one more bird sound to escape.

All morning the image of the bird hung over me like a smudge.

When a crow squawked
loud into the azure summer heat
I could swear

the sound penetrated across continents calling:

Ceasefire!
Ceasefire!

Sam Hamod

There Must be Something Dangerous About a Zoo in Rafah, Palestine

Just yesterday, the Israeli tank
came forward, into the zoo,
firing round
after round, the Cockatoos
screeched, the Macaws went
wild in their cages, screen wire
smithering into thousands of
shreds of death, piercing
the 2 am night air
sending the Raccoon
into panic as his leg
sliced open, and the
Monkey's arm went limp
with the crunch of his tree,
hundreds of Parrots were
caught in a large net
and whisked away in the cab
of a bulldozer, while another
tank shell shattered the
night air, caving in the
roof of the keeper's workshed,
where Mohammad Juma had
worked for months
creating a zoo
for the children of Rafah, the
only recreation
in this nightmare,
of Israeli destruction,
where children weren't allowed
to go out
fearing Israeli snipers,
old lady Khamis
wanted to stay in her house,

bulldozer grinding toward her,
finally her daughter dragged
her, screaming from the
falling wall that covered them both with
cuts and dust, shattering
memories, creating new
sorrows

But this zoo,
there must have been something dangerous
about this zoo, something
that worried the Israelis, perhaps
it was the smiles
it brought to the children's faces

But now,
"The fox has run off," Jumah says,
but no one has any idea where—probably
dug in behind an old shell hole, shivering
from the shaking ground
as the tank grinds up the last of the
bird enclosures—the bulldozer grabs
and grabs and grabs, pushing
the entire scraps
of the defunct zoo
into the swimming pool

the Macaws cry out
mournfully, covering the
wailing of women,
sobbing of the children, the
rage and frustration of Juma
as he picks up what is left
of the sign that says,
"Welcome to Rafah,
Welcome to our Zoo"

Lawrence Ferlinghetti

Cries of Animals Dying

In a dream within a dream I dreamt a dream
of all the animals dying out
all animals everywhere
dying & dying
the wild animals the longhaired animals
winged animals feathered animals
clawed & scaled & furry animals
rutting & dying & dying
in shrinking rainforests
in piney woods and high sierras
on shrinking prairies & tumbleweed mesas
captured beaten starved & stunned
cornered and traded
species not meant to be nomadic
wandering rootless as man
All the animals crying out
in their hidden places
slinking away and crawling away
through the last wild places
through the dense underbrush
the last Great Thickets
beyond the mountains
crisscrossed with switchbacks
beyond the marshes
beyond the plains and fences
(the West won with barbed-wire machines)
in the high country
in the low country
in the bayous
crisscrossed with highways

In a dream within a dream I dreamt
of how they feed & rut & run & hide
how the seals are beaten on ice-fields

the soft white furry seals with eggshell skulls
the great green turtles beaten & eaten
exotic birds netted & caged & tethered
rare wild beasts & strange reptiles & weird woozoos
hunted down for zoos
by bearded black marketeers
who afterwards ride around Singapore
in German limousines
with French whores

In a dream within a dream I dreamt a dream
of all the earth drying up
to a burnt cinder
in the famous Greenhouse Effect
under a canopy of carbon dioxide
breathed out by a billion
infernal combustion engines
mixed with the sweet smell of burning flesh
And all the animals calling to each other
In codes we never understand
The seal and steer cry out
in the same voice the same cry
The wounds never heal
in the commonweal of animals
We steal their lives
to feed our own
and with their lives
our dreams are sown

In a dream within a dream I dreamt a dream
of the daily scrimmage for existence
in the wind-up model of the universe
the spinning meat-wheel world
about to consume itself
And in a dream within a dream I saw
how the bad breath of machines
sickens earth and man
and consumer culture

eats earth and man
and bottom-line capitalism
masquerading as democracy
rapes earth and man

But in a dream I dreamt a dream of how
all the watershed people of the earth
all the ethnic peoples of the earth
all the disenfranchised people of the world
the Mom-and-Pop people of America
the youth of America and the poor of America
would at last rise up
and dismantle industrial civilization
without killing anybody
and save mankind from itself.

Back-up sound: Bird cries, recorded by Mariah Gilardin

Margaret Gibson

Imperative

Don't allow the painful moment to dissolve

Hunt through the nightfall rubble
Bring home what hurts

(Two young men in Palestine
wipe their hands on their khaki shirts)

Hunt through the nightfall rubble
until your voice

has weight in it

Look, it says
(That was a dead Arab child they carried)

Don't say, *Imagine it*. Say, I *see*

(A grief like no other. A child
covered in blood)

D.H. Melhem

Boy in a Hospital

Boy in a hospital
lying among suddenly ancient ruins
that join the Temple of Jupiter
at Baalbek
to the gutted apartments
of Beirut
its buildings glutted
with collapsing life
with bodies
like fragments of statues
newly classical

Boy in a hospital
your olive skin has the pallor of smoke
you have had your moment's attention
there is no sanctuary here there is panic here
the wounded are wounded again

How black your eyes stare into the world
that tore from you
mother father sister brother
tore off your legs

There was no food or water
the walls kept going down
the burning sky kept falling

Boy in a hospital
you are the way to Beirut
the road of pain
the road of shouting corpses
of amputated legs thrown into the street
with newspapers and expectations

to dance the dabke
to share your sister's and brother's laughter
rushing up the stairs
to your apartment
to taste your mother's stuffed grape leaves
from the enamel pot
to run along the beach
your hand safely in your father's

Yasmin Adib

Connecting Flight

In 1982, a group of Lebanese and Palestinian children wounded in the Israeli invasion of Lebanon came to the U.S. for medical treatment. I met Selim in Kennedy Airport on his way back home.

He waits at the gate
for guides
to his connecting flight.
Nine years old
freckled, skinny
in a plaid jacket
and a clip-on tie,
Selim is not
blind
or burned
or missing arms and legs
like the others.

I extend my hand in greeting.
Something shiny flashes from his pocket
and sits heavy in my palm
like a cold wrench.
His eyes, like two green doors
are brightly lit
to ward off robbers,
and acknowledge
my unspoken apologies.

I picture him playing
in the streets of Beirut
finding a shiny splinter
of cluster bomb
that blows off
his right hand
and leaves only the thumb

and forefinger
of his left hand
stretched into a pistol.

Selim hurries through
the airport terminal
ahead of his guides
following an inner radar
calling him home.
He fidgets with a shoulder strap
under his jacket.

I picture him
folding into his mother's flesh
at Beirut airport
tapping her wet cheeks
with his iron fist.

Selim sits impatient
to board his plane.
His left hand
—the pistol—
fixes a Coca Cola can
inside his iron claw.
The aluminum crackles
with every sip
and is crushed when empty.
"Bukra el-Eid," he says in Arabic.
"Tomorrow's the Feast."

Martín Espada

Blues for the Soldiers Who Told You

I'm like a country who can't remember the last war.
—Doug Anderson

They told you that the enemy and the liberated throng
swaddle themselves in the same robes and rags,
wear the same masks with eyes that follow you,
pray in the same bewildering tongue, until your rifle
trembles to rake the faces at every checkpoint.
They told you about the corpse of a boy or girl
rolled at your feet, hair gray with the powder
of rubble and bombardment, flies a whirlpool blackening both eyes,
said you'll learn the words for apology too late to join
the ceremony, as flies become the chorus of your nightmares.
They told you about the double amputee from your town,
legs lopped off by the blast, his basketball friend
bumping home in a flag-draped coffin
the cameras will not film anymore,
about veterans who drench themselves in liquor
like monks pouring gasoline on their heads.

They told you in poems and stories
you did not read, or stopped reading
as your cheeks scorched with inexplicable fever,
and because they spoke with a clarity that burned your face,
because they saw with the vision of a telescope
revolving around the earth, they spent years wandering
through jails and bars, exiled to roads after midnight
where gas stations snap their lights off one by one,
seers unseen at the coffee shop waiting for bacon and eggs,
calling at 3 AM to say *I can't stop writing and you have to hear this.*
You will not hear this, even after the war is over
and the troops drown in a monsoon of desert flowers
tossed by the crowd, blooming in their mouths
to stop their tongues with the sweetness of it.

in this our day of darkness see what beyond the scattered
leaves the Sybil said no time to gape at games the place that
once was across the waters the shores that lie beyond the
blurry lines going away like things spent to live in the very
glint of what little might have been paradise such blood and
dreams there don't seem to be any civilians face about face I
don't care about the imperial mouthpiece doesn't need any face
to fight his war I don't read about that stuff in the line of duty in
the line of destiny without losing control to speculate about
what may or may not be included in a plan that might or might
not be implemented is inappropriate in this secret room drawing
now if to sympathize or if to despise such blood and dreams this
empire of dreams dreaming of empire and blazing fields in the
fearful hearts of such good people heaping much more on their
plates than they can eat these are the innocents over and over
again they claim they have no one to talk to—'rested and
resolute,' 'calm and resigned,' 'determined and vigilant,' 'steady
and strong' a life which does not need war would go up used
like destiny to always learn the passion for the justice things
not sufficiently heroic buildings taken out on the way
to work collapsing in this bitter inheritance of caliber and
alchemy this heaving breast of sleep and horn and ivory

Beirut 2006

My Israeli friend Nachum who is blind
and an expert stone mason tells me
he carries a pistol when he goes back to Nahariya
I'll shoot them all before they kill me
I look at him speechless
cite the lopsided numbers
his face goes blank
he feels my silence
reminds me
I am here, not there,
trying to make peace with the stone

Saladin Ahmed

Beirut

City of leaded fuels and labneh!
City of the scything silver moon!
Make me drunk with your beach-heat!

O muezzin! I hear your call
in the pawn shops of the brown and lonely.
Hashish and Hezb'Allah rallies—
is this my Detroit, come back to me?

This city of purple and pink
flowers like fists,
unnameable trees and clock towers,
everywhere, everywhere,
your bullet holes, your bomb craters—
your pimples, your scars,
this face you
could be beautiful girl.

Nathalie Handal

Beirut

I walk away with your eyes, half-way realize,
I didn't know their color. The way their lashes
move, the color lipstick that makes them stare.
I beg for the shape of glow to reveal itself,
for any presence, for absence we've discovered
has no wind nor song

I look at the leaves on a dry echo,
on a lazy window, by a side door,
look at the rays caught in husky voices
knowing the trembling can't divide our quiet

And we finally understand
what we've missed most about home:
the color of light
the bowls of apricots and grapes
the rose *ahweh* and light moon
the tobacco ash on our floors
the trees that let evening free
and the rhythm of prayers
we will always know,
our eyes shut,
we march
to the anthem under our tongue

Tracie Morris

ochres

in the desiccate earth
water's first to go

from tawny digits, sandysand
colors turned

sienna against bright noon,
unbleachable hue in gravel

freckles, flicked skin
dusts lilt unsettled in air

that looks for all the world, like dand-
ilion. famished huffs in the open

lithe digits pick down
recalled scraps—perhaps tender

additions to slivered lamb
cured color, curled from drying

Elmaz Abinader

Shouldering the Sky

have an easy life, baby

A finger writes a name in the sky
or maybe a planet shoots off a satellite—
when you are born the grandmothers
have told children for centuries, *a star*
appears in the sky, and when you die
it fades. We breathe in galaxies in the gasp
of being celestial, of being a heavenly body

When a child is named Jenin
and enters the world solid large and beautiful
we believe that stars have orbits
and don't leave or fade
but like comets make visitations
to remind us that fire
is the substance of our presence
on this earth.

When a child is named Jenin
she is welcomed by a nation who longs
for the missing, the disappeared, the ones
under a fallen sky, caught between
their land and their lives, poets
interrupted mid-line, words hanging
in the air that we try to catch
before they ascend into the dark night

We prefer finding them above us
we prefer imagining their constellations
the stories they live after they fell
under the crush of their own country
inside the chalky boulders of a village
the craters of a distant moon.

But take heart, here is Jenin
first to air and sky, first to light
and breezes, first to sighs and music
diamond eyes of stars, the cold fire
of history. Jenin, you are new,
you are the salvation of us turning dark
every time we think a star fades or is snuffed out.
You are the story that continues life
after life, birth after birth. Jenin,
you have no purpose in this world
but to carry a name that honors stars
that did not disappear, who are lucky
enough to re-enter the world clutched
in your tiny hands, the silken flowers
reaching upwards, offering their lifelines
to the words, memories, names, songs,
salutations, dreams of many we long
to see again. Jenin, you rebuild us.

Robert Bagg

Bumper Sticker Blues

THE PEOPLE harangues its masters

November 3, 2004

Just call me DEMOS. Ever since Athens
partisan warfare has poisoned my veins.
I switch dysfunctions overnight: I bleed
with macho bluster, then subside toward greed,
disarming nations first *with* steel, then...*of* gold.
I am forever at everyone's mercy—
a groundswell of voters can make me crazy.
You decide—I only do what I'm told.

Plato believed your only sane way out
was rule by some hyper-rational wonk—
but one too decent ever to go wrong.
Now YOU'RE about to MISELECT a lout!
Has terror—*theirs* and *yours*—come on so strong?
IF YOU BELIEVE YOUR VOTE WON'T COUNT, **HONK!**

Sam Hamill

Homeland Security

after Borges

No one is the homeland. The myths of history
cannot clothe the Emperor's nakedness,
no speech empower a vote not counted,
nor honor the living who are impoverished
by our anthems for the dead. No one
is the homeland. Not the heroes of our
old genocides, the Indian Wars, nor those
who sailed west with cargoes of human flesh
in chains, nor those in chains who came
against their will to work and breed and die
in the service of their masters, masters
whose sons would be masters of us all today.

There are no heroes except the ones
who rise to greet the dawn with empty hands
and heavy hearts in a brutal time. No oath
or pledge reveals what's in the heart or mind.
No one is the homeland. Or everyone.
For who lives without a country of the heart?
And yet we cry, "We!" We cry, "Them!"
I pledge allegiance to the kind.
Among the exiled, I make my stand.
No true democracy can be won
at the point of a loaded gun, nor honor found
in anthems or cheap paradigms
based on the social lie. No one is the homeland.

It can't be found in the grandiloquence
of pompous village idiots who run for office
because they want the power. Nor in the brilliance
of the medals on a uniform worn by a man
whose thinking is uniform and obedient
as he swears his pledge of allegiance.
The homeland is a state of grace, of peace,
a whole new world that patiently awaits.
The homeland is a state of mind, a light
flooding the garden, a transcendent moment
of compassionate awareness, one extraordinary line
in some old poem that reveals or exemplifies
a possibility... *in time... in time...*

Becky Thompson

Questions

What is it like, *salat* in the city?

Five times a day, the muezzin's voice
   fog horn the color of sand
calls the men to prayer
   knees leading toward Mecca
the city breathes mosques

What is it like to stand during prayer?

My mind bows with the men
   stays with the women
I want to cover my head
   bend away from the West

What was it like when you died?
My mother calls me home
   come lamb, he is going
my mother's flute singing psalms
   you open your eyes
we are with you, there are circles
   surrounding your bed
rocking we are rocking
   your eyes as big as the sea
you ride smoke rings to the sky
   Arab father now sand

Is there a prayer
   that is upright and kneeling?
Is there a home
   that is not made of glass?

Seema V. Atalla

Optical Illusions

As we toss salad,
bombs are falling.

As we tend roses and geraniums,
metal mangles bodies.

As I lift this fragile blue bowl,
lives shatter.

And years are gone
like a napkin held to a flame.

Khaled Mattawa

Days of 2004

Air that shepherds jet fighters, missiles, drones, how come you've allowed yourself into our lungs, singed, with the dust of our homes, the scent of our loved ones' corpses. Why do you allow us to sip you now, lick you, drink you in heaving gulps?

Your mere wiping of your brow is melodrama.
It drips in your eyes and stings them.
You are drenched, but you've survived,
how not to complain, how not to feel
fate clamping you in his fist. You're a victim;

it's no laughing matter, not even between friends.
It's your turn now to cast another fruitless stone.
The devil on the other side is bemused as you lift
your murdered son to the cameras. A melodrama
What to call it when that's how your life has been.

Not a month has gone since curfew, snipers shooting at any twitch, any shadow, at spring itself that now shivers in branches and grasses, at the silhouette of a woman across a window pane. The bullet that pierced her is now buried with her, an amulet in the jewel box of her heart. The occupants forced to leave their homes, move in with neighbors. The sandbagged roof terraces, the soldiers defecating in kitchen sinks, in pots and pans, on computers, on the beds of the children. The occupied must go on. They've replaced almost all the cracked window panes, the blasted doors, removed the cars that the tanks crushed the way one flattens a soda can with a foot.

Rain that fell on our imprisoned loved ones, dug your cold needles in their skin... And that foul water, warm like blood falling from the soldiers' penises on our heads, our faces, our shoulders and chests, escaping into our mouths. Slide back to your wells and springs, climb back to your clouds. Perform your ablutions, then return.

These roads are for you to gallop through.
Why do you still think you're misunderstood?
These roads will kill you.
Why did you think they would love you?

These seats are for your children to roll in,
to squeal and beg you to drive deeper
into the newly planted forest, the scent
of the pines tugging at you,
tugging at them, promising deliverance.

Why did you think it would be easy?

You see this very moment being
reenacted in slow motion,
a string concerto running over it,
the violin for the childish glee, the cello
for the van ahead of you on the road.

Why did you dig up the olives?
Why did you burn the fields?
Why did you bulldoze their homes?

This too is melodrama.
Did you think you could simply pass them?

They don't let you pass them, and they keep pace with you.

You try to make the car go faster. You try nudge off the road?
How long did you think this road would be yours alone?

They pull their guns
and shoot at you and your children
before you have time
to pull your machine gun
and spray them.

Why was your last gesture a little wave?
What were you trying to tell them?

The spirit prods the body, though the spirit too sees the caverns the abducted and the jailed have forked out of the air. One walks avoiding them like potholes or deep gashes in a field. They float about nonetheless—the remains of a suicide bomber, the remains of his victims zoom about us like bats. Whole corpses sometimes take the shape of boulders obstructing the road. Some are pools of still water, sometimes a gust of wind carries the spent scent of their lives.

What have you to say now,
Earth that never quaked,
never gashed to swallow the
soldiers, or to swallow us into
your dark relief. Earth we've
loved and died for, how long
do you think we'll go on
letting the birds of our souls

steal away from their cages
for their want of you…

There are crusades we can ride, states of solitude that would make the world pass like a speeding train. There are cults to rescue us, rituals, prescriptions. And what would that admission do, that collective acknowledgement when there are no options, when we can't accept, so refuse, anything but perdition as long as that rubbery promise keeps stretching and stretching, that line of crumbs. But of course in the end each of us is alone. Tell yourself you're not alone, tell yourself no one else would bear this suffering. You are not afraid of the world's ending, more that it would go on.

And, how easily you found
us, Fire. Though you spared
our great father, you stood
will-less in our enemy's
hands, how you've survived
rain and wind thick with
sand. We will stop naming
our children after you...

Lawrence Ferlinghetti

At La Puerta Escondida

And heard the birds that sound like bells

Lost in the foliage

Among the jacaranda trees

And then ran down to the pool

Overhung with vines

Where you lay bare in a hammock

Your flesh like ripe papaya

And the sun
                    the sun cried out
                                        as it set—
"Again I have not succeeded
                    in burning down the world—
What fire-proofing
                    those lovers must have!"

Kathy Engel

Words Only

I will not write another poem about war.
Pretend I can carve light
out of darkness.

I will not attempt to translate
shrapnel infiltrating a child's body,
bulldozed everything—

methodical process
of taking human identity
the way you suck dust with a vacuum.

I will not make a list of places.

I will not write another poem about war.

I will take a hammer
to break down walls.
I will look for the flowers, 24 years later,
surviving women of Beirut held in their hands—
as they walked away from their charcoaled city,
their husbands' ghosts following.

Frank Reeve

For the Christmas Dead

The situation in Iraq, with armed militarized factions fighting for their own political agendas, can now be characterized as civil war.

—NBC News, November 27, 2006

soft weather we had all fall
the rain   exceeding itself, then hard
          dogging the fox to earth
the snow on Mt. Kenya dying
the sun in its fairy-tale setting
          drowned in a blood-red sea

the crèche is umber; blue
for a sky, a dress, a child's eyes;
          no one includes the smell
of the animals or the air
at Golgotha three days old:
          each death draws closer to Hell

bells in the village church
ring the angels' caroling
          glass notes falling like men
such sorrow, so little joy
as if the world were real
          from beginning to end

PART TWO

And Not Surrender

1982

THE THREE MAGIS —

INTRODUCTION

The following introduction was originally published in And Not Surrender, *Arab American Cultural Foundation, Washington, DC, 1982.*

The politician wants man to learn how to die with courage; the poet wants him to live with courage." These words by Salvatore Quasimodo pertain to literary traditions in which poetry has often been written directly from the battlefronts. Until very recently, most poets of social and political commitments in the United States have often been suspect in literary circles; after all, trenches have not been a part of the American landscape. However, since the electronic media seems to have become more and more of a reflexive extension of our awareness, opening windows that bring in the vivid apparitions of the war in Vietnam, the so-called battlefronts have been extended to the privacy of the American home. In time, a new shift has taken place in the way political poetry began to be received in this country.

As news reporters claimed to objectify reality, the American poet's role continued to subjectify it. "More than the European," Stephen Spender once explained, "the American writer *exists* in his fiction or poetry. In his work, objective material becomes subjective, whereas in English poetry or fiction, the subjective becomes objectified."[1] This very kind of subjectivity criticized by Spender has traditionally been central to the American literary expression. However, during the last few decades this subjectivity has been instrumental in transcending the borders of provinciality, bringing the humanity of a world thousands of miles away into the American literary language, thus furthering American literary sensibility. Whitman once declared, "to be a poet is to commensurate with a people... presidents shall not be their common referee so much as their poets shall." This modest anthology of poems is an attempt to illustrate this one aspect of America's poetic tradition today.

The works of the 19 poets here form an unusual compilation of well-known poets next to unfamiliar names.

[1] Stephen Spender, *Love-Hate Relations: English and American Sensibilities* (Random House, 1974), 21.

Some poets are represented with one or two poems, others with as many as four or five. With the exception of works by two poets, all poems included have been written within the last four months. The collection does not attempt to illustrate individual fragments of one voice in contrast to another; rather, it stresses the chorality of poetry, as it focuses on the unfolding of a human drama. Here, 18 poets in America and a Canadian pour out feelings they experienced between June and September of 1982, as they watched in live color Lebanon's frontlines being crushed under the advancing tanks of America's closest ally.

In this collection of poems, the electronic media is not adjunctive to the written word, because it is not merely a causative element in the making of this poetry. It constitutes a more organic element in the innate qualities of the works. The cinematic brevity and sudden cuts of a visual nature that we experience in a news story are as much a part of the poetry's cadence as the brief expression in a news dispatch is. In our minds, the papery feel of a newspaper is contrasted to the warmth of human skin, just as the sound of a radio announcer bolts the thunder of exploding bombs, and the glaring light of a television screen stands like a wall separating "us" from "them." Contrasts accentuating the "here" from the "there" translate to contrasts between memory and apprehension, between motion and stillness, between rest and strife.

On "a photogray day" in Washington, D.C., Chris Llewellyn, getting ready to jog, "sp[ies] a pile of *Posts* packed under mailbox... pictures of shredded skies..."; she remembers "a near stranger and continents away," a Palestinian who as a child fled with his family in a train, on its way the train was blown up, Llewellyn goes on, "running... running..."

Samuel Hazo in Pittsburgh is driving a car. The night has fallen, "a dashboard voice from Washington/ talks war in Lebanon... / bursting like rocketry, a scar of fire/ slashes down the sky "; he remembers Lorca and thinks of "this Guernica in Beirut..."

As she is breathing the "thin air" of a peaceful summer day in the Adirondacks, Sara Miles is "thinking: homeland/ past the old rock walls grown green with vine hearing/ jets roar low over other hills of home and it must be/ almost night now in that land"; she wonders "if the bombing has started yet."

Kathy Engel in New York City sits in front of the television set watching "as the camera pulls back/ and the screams follow/ switching channels incessantly/ to get each news on each station/ with each commentator/with combed hair and the language of war/... many numbers and no names... / ... We can't get close enough/ pushing our faces up against the smudged screen... / one fly buzzes across the cool surface/ and there— flies upon flies swarm."

In California, Etel Adnan writes that even in Beirut "Muhammad is confused/ he hallucinates/ each night/ in front of the radio/ and vomits the news." She asks, "Do you know/ that people [in Beirut] were not running in a nightmare but in/ front of television?"

Given the controversy that arose over conflicting reports on the exact number of casualties, and the way the media portrayed the two opponents in this drama, the American poets could not stand idle. Sara Miles writes in "And Not Surrender," "It gets worse: all the newspapers make/ the same lie the television the stories separating us/ each from each other/ calling this one terrorist/ this one refugee/ this one Brooklyn resident, twenty nine/ I am flesh of that flesh/ reconstructing." Kathy Engel, knowing she may speak "from the heart/ with inadequate documentation" writes "To the Editor" asking, "shall I send a human limb wrapped in brown paper/ or tape record overseas phone calls/ with the sound of human wailing?" June Jordan, angry at having to list atrocities and their counter claims, tells us in another poem that on those two sides of the barbed wire "the world is neither yours nor mine." In fusing the self with the other, she declares, "I was born a black woman and now/ I am become a Palestinian." James Scully, having witnessed how an atrocious military invasion in the words of such respectable American intellectuals as William Safire is described as "Israel liberating Lebanon" (*New York Times*, June 11, 1982), turns the English language around and begins by speaking about the Soviet invasion of Afghanistan, to explain how really "only the names have changed."

On a more intimate level, where personal memory meets with the apprehensions of the news bulletin, Denise Levertov, the daughter of a harmonious union between a Jewish father and a Welsh mother, is in Massachusetts writing "a libretto/ about El Salvador the suffering/ the martyrs/ look[s] from [her] page to watch/ the apportioned news—those foul/ dollops of History." She remembers her parents, whom she misses, and laments, "Now I see/ it is well you are dead," spared from seeing fragments of this "Age of Terror." In Texas, Naomi Shihab Nye, the daughter of a Palestinian father and an American mother, writes, "today the headlines clot in my blood" she sees "a little Palestinian dangles a truck on the front page...I call my father, we talk around the news/ It is too much for him/ neither of his two languages can reach it." She goes out in the open "to plead with the air."

Back in a mountainous region in Lebanon, a soldier boy by the name of Yaron Zamir falls. Before he was sent to conquer the castle of Beaufort, he attempted to articulate some feelings he had written in Hebrew: "And this small thing—a world of hatred/ with the same people and with a song of protest/ can now stand up and rebel and cry out to the world *enough! don't kill*." His father, Yehosua Zamir, who lives in Galilee, wrote to a newspaper, "What can I say to the [Arab] neighbor who came to console me after my son Yaron fell on the same day that my neighbor's family was bombed in Sidon?" (*Al-Hamishmar*, July 1, 1982; *Village Voice*, July 20, 1982).

In the mountains in upstate New York while the war is going on, we were two Jews and two Arabs going to visit David Truong, an old friend from Vietnam, now serving a sentence in a federal prison, "We fill in pink slips/ to visit a man in prison who tried/ to stop a war in his country."

Miles protests, "The war/ isn't tragic/ it's wrong." Engel laments "in the country of our untrained voices/ if only we knew a way... / to stop this war"; she painfully admits "our only real weapon/ is the heart and the howl/ that comes from it." The Lebanese-born Etel Adnan howls, "poets go home/ unless you change the world!" but then recognizing that the only companions of the victimized "are the poets of/ Russia and America/ And the Indians of Guatemala," she extols, "those who fight/ with their fists/ against airplanes."

This summer in Washington, D.C. I remember feeling that helplessness during a demonstration against the Israeli invasion of Lebanon. A long time friend, Ellen Siegel, expressed to me her sense of frustration, saying she ought to go to Lebanon to offer her services as a nurse. Later I learned that Ellen was in Sabra when, as Yasmin Adib writes, "they surround[ed] us/ bearing lanterns/ on a New Year's/ sacrificial feast:/ a festival of light/... and their bright light/ that leaves no shadow/ snares a woman/ shot in the back,/ the baby/ raised in her arms,/ shot through the head/... the naked eyes/ of a girl stunned/ by the glare of the light/ stunned/ though they were used to/ death." This same light, which enabled butchers to find their victims, was the only light coming through the hospital window allowing Ellen Siegel, a Jew from Washington, D.C., to help preserve the life of whomever she could.[2]

The Talmud teaches, "Who can protest and does not, is an accomplice in the act" (*Sabbath, 54b*); perhaps the voices of the Jewish poets in this collection are most illustrative of this. Barbara Berman, brought up not to forget "the lessons of the Six Million/ whose dust we all share" she retorts, "they say for the sake of the green Galilee they will kill in my name." Gabrielle Edgcomb, "German Jew/ survivor from Berlin before the last round-up," declares her "rage against all man made massacres" and warns "they're rounding up again/ and still." Kathy Engel questions, "Does it say/ in the Old Testament somewhere:/ kill your neighbors?" And when I told Kathy of Tony Abdelnour, a Lebanese University professor who was shot at the doorstep of his house in Bhamdoun shortly after the town fell into the hands of the Israeli army, Kathy could see "a flash light in the door/ a man pulled in the road, a shot"; she asks, "it happened before like that/ remember?"

It could have been in Vietnam, it could have been in Germany, Dennis Lee does not look for differences. He looks at the screen of a television set and sees a different picture; he

[2] Ellen Siegel, "After 19 Years: Sabra and Shatila Remembered," *Middle East Policy Journal* VIII.4 (December 2001).

reminds us, "the earth, our infinite planet/ is growing small... //It is time—time that the race/ of the beings who dwell on earth/ imagine their death...// yet we *are*/ one race: the race of beings/ that will perish together if planet earth is destroyed,/ and if Sabra prevails/ the story of Sabra will be the story of earth/... / Our enemies are those who do not recognize/ our painful, shared community./ We must know them well/after Sabra.../ after Shatila..."

As this book goes to press, poems that could be included are still arriving in the mail. The camera crews have long withdrawn from the battlefield. The occupying armies have not. Poetry shall go on "...despite/ the wind, despite the worst." In this chorale that asserts the courage to live and that tells us what living feels like, the "antennas of the race," as Ezra Pound described the poets, will tomorrow: "remind each other: It begins here, with this caring, this fullness of care."

—Kamal Boullata

Washington, D.C.
November 18, 1982

Sara Miles

And Not Surrender

It gets worse: all the newspapers make
the same lies the television the stories separating us
each from each other
calling this one terrorist
this one refugee
this one Brooklyn resident, twenty-nine.
I am flesh of that flesh
reconstructing:
touching the skin of my leg with its charred scar
red and tender still a year later and watching
the news where a thirteen-year old girl
on the white hospital bed in Beirut kicks
helplessly kicks her legs and the burning won't stop.
And it gets worse: we sink
in this room in late summer thinking
what can we do? and fail to think hard enough
ashamed
desperate
hating our helplessness among the clippings
the lying newspapers angry letters
notebooks photos and lists: bitterness
of inadequate imagination while
the girl goes on beating her legs against the bed
flesh of my flesh
how we lose each other
this is the worst. Try. To raise
the eyes, turn off the television
gaze at some real body as if love
could invent intelligence enough to save love—
As love
made me heal, and stand up
and walk into this room a year later
to hurt again
to speak now
to make the burning stop.

June Jordan

Apologies to All the People in Lebanon

Dedicated to the 600,000 Palestinian men, women and children who have lived in Lebanon since 1948

I didn't know and nobody told me and what
Could I do or say, anyway?

They said you shot the London ambassador
And when that wasn't true
They said so
What
They said you shelled their northern villages
And when U.N. forces reported that was not true
Because your side of the cease fire was holding
Since more than a year before
They said so
What
They said they wanted simply to carve
A 25 mile buffer zone and then
They ravaged your
Water supplies your electricity your
Hospitals your schools your highways and byways all
The way north to Beirut because they said this
Was their quest for peace
They blew up your homes and demolished the grocery
Stores and blocked the Red Cross and took away doctors
To jail and they cluster-bombed girls and boys whose bodies
Swelled purple and black into twice their original size
And tore the buttocks from a four-month old baby and then
They said this was brilliant
Military accomplishment and this was done
They said in the name of self-defense they said
That is the noblest concept
Of mankind isn't that obvious?
They said something about never again and then

They made close to one million human beings homeless
In less than three weeks and they killed or maimed
40,000 of your men and your women and your children

But I didn't know and nobody told me and what
Could I do or say, anyway?

They said they were victims. They said you were
Arabs.
They called your apartments and gardens guerilla
Strongholds.
They called the screaming devastation
That they created the rubble
Then they told you to leave, didn't they?
Didn't you read the leaflets that they dropped
From their hotshot fighter jets?
They told you to go.
One hundred and thirty-five thousand
Palestinians in Beirut and why
Didn't you take the hint?
Go!
There was the Mediterranean: You
Could walk into the water and stay
There.
What was the problem?

I didn't know and nobody told me and what
Could I do or say, anyway?

Yes I did know it was the money I earned as a poet that paid
For the bombs and the planes and the tanks
That they used to massacre your family

But I am not an evil person
The people of my country aren't so bad

You can't expect but so much

From those of us who have to pay taxes and watch
American TV

You see my point.

I'm sorry
I really am sorry

Samuel Hazo

The World That Lightning Makes

Under an upside-down
    and sooty ocean, I steer
    through summer thunder
    and the straight prose of rain.
A dashboard voice from Washington
    talks war in Lebanon...
                        Bursting
    like rocketry, a scar of fire
    slashes down the sky
                        It noons
    the night and shocks me
    to a crawl.
                        My car's a shelter
    under siege.
                        The mean buttons
    of approaching headlights
    change into the always searching
    always aiming eyes of condors.
The lashing rainfall wails
    in Arabic for this Guernica
    in Beirut...
                        I think of Lorca
    who believed the lightning-worlds
    of love and poetry could have
    no enemies.
                        He never dreamed
    of lightning-chevrons on black
    shirts, lightning-wars
    and lightning-zigzags crayoned
    on a map that sparked a war
    that scarred a generation...
                        This
    generation's condors thunder on another
    Spain.

The rain's a litany
of Lorcas bulldozed into pits.
The voice from Washington is no one's
and the world's.
Viva la muerte!

Kathy Engel

Letter to the Editor

Dear friend, I must have been mistaken
to mourn those lives lost
without the proper data or permission
to accurately claim them:
real, necessary, losses at all?
I must have been out of my head
to feel a responsibility
for a people without a place to live
hunted down by my people
who were without a place to live
hunted down.

Dear Editor: I know it is wrong
in the technological age
to speak from the heart
with inadequate documentation—
shall I send a human limb wrapped in brown paper
or tape record overseas phone calls
with the sound of human wailing?

Dear readers: I know I had no right
from far away, without a degree
in war, weaponry or even history
to indicate there is any way to peace
but war
blood answers blood
a tank of prejudice fuels us
and the unfortunates lost along the way are history's
punctuation, unnecessary appendages—
wildflowers perhaps.

We live in the body of our history
and drink the blood of our ancestors

and it is preposterous I know to think
we might harden
towards those who resemble us
in their fears
like the child beaten by her mother
and she watches herself growing again
and sees something so familiar
in that young face, in a gesture,
so terrifying that her impatience and fury
rise in her
like a jackhammer
for all she suffered, for all she lost and endured
without quite knowing what she is doing
her arms let loose across her child's face
and back and legs
as if the beating could unleash her past
and she hates herself for hurting
who she loves
and she hates who she loves
for reminding her
and the guilt and anger
gather within her
the energy to do it again.

Dear respondent: I know that you know
that someone knows
exactly what he's doing and I am sure
that you are correct in your analysis,
I am politically naïve
I do believe
that unless we find another way
to live together
we will all die together
each alone

in all our grand sophistication
the banks will close
unwillingly, with scores of footnotes

and theoretical explanations
but the buildings themselves
will remain in their glory.

Dear historian: Please show me
the legacy of proof
tangible as barbed wire
unlike the failure of imagination
that has brought us here.
Show me the pattern of victory
that marvels at the human spirit.
Explain how to ask the question in the informed fashion.

Dear sisters: please stand by me
I know this is a diatribe
I have insubstantial proof for my thesis
being a woman
I demand
love and support, rely too much
on instinct, feelings and irrational
passions: like they say a bad weed
grows back whenever you dig it up
maybe we'll just have to
practice preventive killing
God knows it would clarify things.
Maybe we could do it—beautifully.

Dear lover: we are talking about
necessary defense strategies,
remember when you were afraid to say:
I love you?

Gabrielle S. Edgcomb

Letter from Mona Saudi:
Beirut Summer 1982

We have not lost our hope
the garden these warm days is beautiful
sculptures grow like flowers
wait as we wait

dear friend I ask one favor
keep the slides

this note sounds like a will
forgive me for that please

the planes roar overhead
machine guns clatter
the garden beautiful
sculptures grow
wait

Pablo Medina

Bombing of Tyre

We've left the children out
again, torn fences down,
made caverns where the gardens
grew. Look at them watch cinders,

eyes sparkling with vacant
flames, despair. Blast me
if I know what these stones mean
except that men once shaped them

to escape. And he of stones
came strutting by: "Bombs and man,
the bursting heart"
then into the flashing sea.

We found this:
land drove us skyward
with our pillared dreams.
Bones of our fathers

gathered at the edge of town
where the road leads long away;
the land is lost
to the lapping waves,

the passion of the saints
maims labor with silence here:
wandering in dust
for forty years.

Learn to recognize the pride
we bring to peristyles
and colonnades. It crumbles.

Learn the pieces falling.

Make room in the heart:
the moon dye spills. Who knows?
So many ruins
and the sparkle of fire in boys' eyes.

Denise Levertov

Perhaps No Poem But All I Can Say And I Cannot Be Silent

As a devout Christian, my father
took delight and pride in being
(like Christ and the Apostles)
a Jew.
            It was
            Hasidic lore, his heritage,
            he drew on to know
            the Holy Spirit as Shekinah.

My Gentile mother, Welsh through and through,
and like my father sustained
by deep faith, cherished
all her long life the words
of Israel Zangwill, who told her,
'You have a Jewish soul'.

I, their daughter ('flesh of their flesh,
                              bone of their bone')
writing, in this Age of Terror, a libretto
about El Salvador the suffering,
                              the martyrs,

look from my page to watch
the apportioned news—those foul
dollops of History
each day thrusts at us, pushing them
into our gullets—
                              and see that,
                              in Lebanon

            so-called Jews have permitted
            so-called Christians

to wreak pogrom ('thunder of devastation')
on helpless folk (of a tribe
anciently kin to their own, and now
concentrated
in Camps...)

My father—my mother—
I have longed for you.
Now I see
it is well you are dead,
dead and
gone from Time,
gone from this time whose weight
of shame your bones, weary already
from your own days and years of
tragic History,
could surely not have borne.

Blood

"A true Arab knows how to catch a fly in his hands,"
my father would say. And he'd prove it,
cupping the buzzer instantly
while the host with the swatter stared.

In the spring our palms peeled like snakes.
True Arabs believed watermelon could heal fifty ways.
I changed these to fit the occasion.

Years before, a girl knocked,
wanted to see the Arab.
I said we didn't have one.
After that, my father told me who he was,
"Shihab"—"shooting star"—
a good name, borrowed from the sky.
Once I said, "When we die, we give it back?"
He said that's what a true Arab would say.

Today the headlines clot in my blood.
A little Palestinian dangles a truck on the front page.
Homeless fig, this tragedy with a terrible root
is too big for us. What flag can we wave?
I wave the flag of stone and seed,
table-mat stitched in blue.

I call my father, we talk around the news.
It is too much for him,
neither of his two languages can reach it.
I drive into the country to find sheep, cows,
to plead with the air:
Who calls anyone *civilized?*
Where can the crying heart graze?
What does a true Arab do now?

James Scully

The Soviet Union Invades Afghanistan

When the Soviet Union invades Afghanistan, the Soviet Union invades Afghanistan.

When Israel invades Lebanon, Israel does not invade Lebanon. Israel liberates Lebanon. The operation is called Peace for Galilee.

It takes many corpses to make this peace. Many arms, legs, eyes. Arms to be raised or lowered, legs to crouch running, eyes not to see. And it takes many ceasefires. When the Israelis declare a ceasefire, all west Beirut scurries for shelter from the bombs and shells that are sure to follow.

Israel liberates Lebanon from armed Palestinian refugees who live near people. Near Lebanese, who live in the way of Israeli bombs. Even nearer their own families, also in the way. This demonstrates Palestinian cynicism: They wrap themselves in their mothers' skirts. Now, to get at Palestinians armed to protect the refugee camps they and their families live in, the Israelis must shell helpless civilians. Why don't the refugees live somewhere else? Why don't they go home? as a midwestern American reporter put it. Why must they live among people?

On Israeli news, Palestinian refugees are terrorists. Not men, women, babies, farmers, auto mechanics, secretaries, school kids, girls washing clothes, peddlers, nurses, guerrillas. Including, doubtless, some suicide commando terrorists. No, like any epidemic, homeless Palestinians are without exception international terrorists. That's why the

Israeli army must imprison their doctors, cutting off water, electricity, food and medical supplies.

Israel harbors no terrorists. Menachem Begin and Ariel Sharon are not international terrorists. They are Prime Minister and Defense Minister, respectively, of the state of Israel. Yitzhak Shamir is the Foreign Minister. They have not gotten where they are, to become respectable, by blowing up hotels or massacring innocent villagers in Qibya, in Deir Yassin and elsewhere.

This very morning, 4 August 1982, Prime Minister Begin announced, to laughter and clapping from 200 visiting Americans come to support the invasion, that soon he'll be offering package tours of Lebanon, that already at the northern Israeli border there's a tourist boom. "Their hotels are 100% full," he said. "It should only happen to the Waldorf Astoria." Does this sound like international terrorism? He even keeps his word. During the siege of Beirut he sends busloads of tourists to sightsee the new ruins of Sidon.

But before tourists arrive in force, Palestinians must be gotten rid of. Naturally it is not enough to kill them. They must be annihilated philosophically as well. Like "two-legged beasts." So as Begin and Sharon pursue this extermination-and-dispersal policy into Beirut and beyond—not counting Palestinians or goats or shredded orange groves in the death toll, but invoking god and the bible and metaphysical genetic superiority over common humanity—their banner of sordid sacred righteousness is raised over the mortified illusions of those innocents who believed fascism had to be German or other, and that victims of racism could not themselves commit racist murder.

For when Israeli soldiers in Sidon methodically beat
certain prisoners to death, tying ankles to wrists
behind the back and lashing the human bundle to a
tree, who was so principled as to ask: if not
Nuremburg, where will the war crimes trials be
held after *this* war? and who will hold them?

In Tel Aviv 70,000 Israelis with the passionate humane
courage of their, our, history protest all this, as
Hassidim too hold back, they will not go along, nor
will the young Colonel Eli Geva who resigns, and
these confirm that history as warm and precious
as an arm an eye a leg

Yet you are left behind as events pass them by—as the
basket of amputated Lebanese and Palestinian limbs
in a basement field hospital under Beirut is also left
behind, unable to stop the slaughter, for nothing of
this or any historical witness will kick or wave or
make anything happen ever again as it looks on,
horrified.

But what do they behold? How did they understand what
was going on?

For when Begin and Sharon (with their bosses officers
and colonial administrators) hired rightwing Moslem
goon squads and Christian Phalangist gangs
modeled on the Hitler Youth of the 30s, and when
they squeezed patriotic anguish and fear from
Israeli workers, taxing money iron and blood to pay
for this, and shelled not only Palestinian refugee
camps but other wretched working neighborhoods,
theirs was not the army of a chosen people or a
master race nor of the Jews, but the old pitiless
army of class war daily pounding the rubble of the
irrepressible poor

including, in time, the pacifists, the socialists, the trade unionists and always at the end of the line, now momentarily confused, the darker impoverished oriental Jews of Israel, too.

For when that army overruns refugee camps and bulldozes what shelters are left, it wants the homeless without a country to be homeless without a roof, a kitchen, a corner to sleep in. It wants those homeless scattered across the earth, homeless as flies which it may spray and swat with cluster bombs and white phosphorous, whose one purpose is to cut and burn human flesh.

They do not even eat this flesh. Only destroy, destroy, destroy: leaving this for anti-semites to feast on, like maggots, who are the camp followers and secret agents of General Sharon, Ariel Sharon, the butcher with the name of god's lioness, of altars, of plains and Arabian gazelle, who thrusts and lunges from cabinet meetings to carnage in his body of a lumbering toad.

And the worst is, the ordinary boyish graying Israeli soldier is not killing flies. From the hills and gun emplacements around the city, he is pounding and crushing his speck of a brother, a sister, his father mother his own children, it is his own death he is obeying, holding his ears, observing it from a distance. The silence is sickening.

As, the quest for a final solution is carried on by those who endured to prove triumphant there is none. For what have they sacrificed? To make a homeland creating endless homelessness. Then why are they closing ranks? To force another diaspora.

Only the names have changed.

Chris Llewellyn

For Adnan

Scores of Palestinians Killed in Beirut Camps
—Washington Post

A photogray day. Pull on sweatpants,
shirt, double-tie shoes. Toe-touch,
calf-stretch, jumping jacks. I jog
the hall where carpet flowers close
and open, skip down steps' accordion.
Spy a pile of *Posts* packed under mailbox.

And now pain swells midriff, lungs
open and close like peace accords:
... homes dynamited, bulldozed
... rampage extends to babies in diapers
... shoes, toys, horse and sheep corpses
... to the south a large pit bears
markings of a mass grave. And now

Shoes, sheep, horse, I'm running, running
the clay canal with bloody banks, water
pictures of shredded skies. Shoes pound
the spun globe, ground water runs to
oceans, runs to continents. I recall
pastel Atlas pages, how the Key translates
rainfall, elevations, depressions.
And New Testament maps of tissue paper,
the Holy Land, Christ's life and time in
Palestine, (their Legends mark His miracles.)
Fifth grade history texts taught holocaust,
Auschwitz, Dachau. Ten, sick, scared,
I find genocide in the dictionary. In
high school, I hear Yevtuschenko's *Babi Yar*
his Russian tongue recites machine gun,

death march, markings of a mass grave. And
now September Nineteen, another Anno Domini,
I write this poem for you, a near
stranger and continents away.

A near stranger and continents away,
you say: I'm from Haifa, Trans-Jordan,
Syria, West Beirut. We left all belongings
in our farmhouse, animals in barns believing
we'd be back a few days later. Father took
my brothers in a wagon. Mother and I waited,
boarded the train. We ate pine nut cakes
and pocket bread, watched the sun set over
a ridge. While climbing a hill, a huge
thunder spun our car upside down... Parcels
flew, seats shredded . . .glass and metal
blew . . .an arm and foot fell into our
basket. . .soldiers shouting in aisles. . .
rifles and sticks push and hit as if
we were worse than animals
...Ten, sick, scared,

I'm running. . . running. . .

D.H. Melhem

To My Unknown Sister in Beirut

Sister unknown sister
your voice reaches me
from cedars shrouded
in the rubble of your house
and from your thirsty streets
that drink blood
and bake bodies
like loaves of flat bread
tossed into the sun

Sister unknown sister
our fearful brother brings bombs
our brother who bought death
from my father
our brother who ate the blood-lust
of his tormentors
He ate their defeat
and they took his victory

And the song of his fighter jets
screams   screams
the voices of children who were singing
a people proud to be peaceful

Sister unknown sister
whose dark eyes shadow my escape
are the olives bitter
in your throat?
Their pits embarrass
politicians
Your innocence embarrasses
politicians
Your agony embarrasses
politicians

Sister my sister
there are lessons
to be learned
from death

Kathy Engel

I Hold You Responsible for Everything You Do in My Dreams

It is the moon's prerogative
to crank open the night.
The heart gives no permission.
The sheets on the bed are cock-eyed.
I don't need to know how much
you love me, just how.
Boats move out of the harbor
each morning like parents
leaving for work. These murders
rise out of the waters like waves:
It is July, hot, and across
the ocean bombs crack over
people's homes. Blood
in the fire. The sky turns
over. No turn of phrase
can turn it away. No
tongue can give it up.
We can paddle across the lake.
We can sail to the village.
We can turn the motor and go faster.
We can sit on the wooden raft
watch the shadows drop
like a hand over the mountain
and imagine unknown tribes on the other side.
But how can we talk to each other?
An expensive silence fizzes
between us. Just let it go
you always say. We investigate
a nest of swallows. I don't
believe that everything wants a name.
Apple blossoms infuse the air
breaking the path. What is the

geography of this language we live by:
country, city, other? Where does one
locate: homelessness, chased by fear
into cruelty, too many dead
to count, or name?
The canoe takes two: one paddle
for each embracing the water,
dipping down, unlearning borders.
Treeshadows elongate as dusk hits.
What time is it? There? Another bomb.
If only we knew a way
in the country of our untrained voices
with their disparate clamor
to stop this war.
Mosquitoes suck in the blood of night.
Where there is heat and trees and water.
Children. We fill in pink slips
to visit a man in prison who tried
to stop a war in his country.
He is far from home
without boat or paddle.
Where there was heat and trees and water.
His name rests there in duplicate
like a gravestone, for protection.

Sam Hamod

At Fakhani, the Shoe

for Greg Orfalea, who was there

It is a
shoe—a
single baby's
shoe
I pull it from the
wreckage in Fakhani, a refugee
shoe
separated from its
foot, it is April
and it is darkening in the covering
black Lebanese earth, the soft earth
has cracked its white surface, marked with
streaks of blood.

And who wore this shoe, what
little girl, or was it a
boy, what did the
father say when he
smiled, did he laugh
back, or was she a shy girl who had
already learned to be a
coquette—or was she
chubby and withdrawn among
people, if he was a boy
was he already strong, his
dark hair flying as he
wrestled his father's
arm—and what
did her mother say to her
father when they heard the airplanes
screech across the sky, did they hear

the whistle, or was it an
offshore song, Israeli sirens at
sea who sent in wave after wave of
glistening silver sheets of
sorrow

And why was
this little shoe
left by itself to wonder
in the dark, to find its way
to the surface by itself, and how
did it feel
leaving its foot behind—
and what did the foot say
as the shoe slipped away
in the darkness
toward the surface, did the
child turn over as if in
a dream did he dream his
mother and father were blowing
away

And what am I
to say, a stranger now
to my parent's land, in the
bright Washington afternoon,
here in Fakhani, holding onto this
little shoe, feeling grief in
Arabic saying it in English, so
that it is so flat against
the round care of this shoe, something
is missing, how did this shoe come
to surface today to meet me, the
child who can explain it is
sleeping under the new coming
grass, under the splintered
boards and shining glass, and how
long can we stand in the

shadow hiding what our hearts know—like
a telegraph beacon repeating
someone is missing
someone is missing
someone is missing

Now sucking in the air
we drink Palestine, we taste
Lebanon, we hear Syria, we
remember Jordan, all the same
land, the home of the same shoes,
split now like this foot
from its shoe, the blood smell
coming from the piles of debris
in the hot Lebanese sun, and
so we are at home, tearing away
the language and names of countries,
tearing away the memory of these
past two weeks, believing this shoe
never had a foot, something lost
from a shoe store, something made
alone and single in the tannery of
Rafik Dibbs in Machgara in southern
Lebanon, some sort of dream of what it
was like in Aley and Zahle when people
would stay up until early in the morning
doing the dabkeh, eating olives and
kibbeh by the flowing creek

a place where there were
no airplanes, a place where
there were no rockets, no
ships lobbing in shells from
the blue and glistening Mediterranean
Sea—but this shoe, we know
is missing its foot
shall we search in Tel Aviv, in
Washington, in Moscow, shall we

search, or shall we make another
speech, shall we make another
poem, shall we empty the canister
of language and simply
cry.

The shoe
yes
I give you this
shoe
it is
not mine
it is
ours.

June Jordan

To Sing a Song of Palestine

for Shula Koenig
Israeli Spokesperson for the Israeli Peace Now Movement, 1982

All the natural wonders that don't grow there
(Nor tree nor river nor a great plains lifting grain
or grass nor rooted fruit and
vegetables) forever curse the land
with wildly dreaming schemes
of transformation
military magic
thick accomplishments of blood

I sing of Israel and Palestine:
The world as neither yours nor mine:
How many different men will fit
themselves how fast
into that place?

A woman's body as the universal
shelter to the demon or the sweet as paradigm
of home that starts and ends with face
to face surrendering to the need
that each of us can feed or take
away amazing as the space created
by the mothers of our time
—can we behold ourselves
    like that
the ribs the breathing muscles and the fat
of everything desire requires
for its rational abatement?

I write beside the rainy sky
tonight an unexpected an American

cease-fire to the burning day
that worked like war across my
empty throat before I thought to try this way
to say I think we can: I think we can.

Barbara Berman

At the Edge

There is talk of sending troops to the edge.
Again to the edge. And I sit on the edge
of my chair, my comfortable stuffed blue chair.
I do not want to think about comfort,
or about my morning, working with clay
gathered from some peaceful ground;
My afternoon spent rewriting a story
begun two years ago about something that happened
ten years ago, when we didn't question
surviving the next ten years.

And I sit on the edge of my chair.
I think of the edges of houses, balconies, roofs
falling above women and children, "bodies horribly maimed,"
say the nurses, in tears, and all, I am told
for the sake of the green Galilee, so rich, and so green
that bodies are buried beneath the edges of houses.

We come to the edge, for this, the edge
where the voice of a Norwegian doctor breaks
and I leave the room in tears, because
as another Jew has said, "We are here
because our souls ache," and we are at the edge.
No. We have crossed the edge of decency
for the sake of the Galilee we're told by men
who care nothing for deep green hills,
but are proud that American weapons have proved
so efficient at killing women and children
and other men who want nothing of war, and all
for the sake of the Galilee, and all
to prove the superiority of American technology
and forget so quickly the lessons of the Six Million
whose dust we all share, they say for the sake
of the green Galilee they will kill in my name.

Gregory Orfalea

The Bomb That Fell on Abdo's Farm

The Phantoms approached, we were told,
like warps in the sky, like gossip
gone real, aimed in steel
at the eyes of the village.

All the farmers and farmers' boys ran
to the rooftops and watched,
for it was terrifying
and beautiful to see a wedge
of silver up from the South.

And they began to fall with a
vengeance, under the anti-air-
craft that ringed Damascus and the
villagers whooped for there seemed
a magic field around their fields.

Until a cow-shed flew in red to the sky.
And a mother milking collapsed
in her milk. The milk ran pink.

Nextdoor, in my great-uncle's newly-
irrigated fields, a bomb fell.
The mud smothered it. The mud
talked to it. The mud wrapped
its death like a mother. And
the bomb with American lettering
did not go off.

Water your gardens always. Always.

Etel Adnan

Beirut 1982

O the gentle wilderness of the
heart
the day Beirut died under
a shower of red flowers!

Um Kalsum had left us first:
she used to sing for angels and horses...
Then silent Palestinians followed
her
in procession
like in the frescoes of their
ancestors
The Beasts are not in the Zoos...

B for Begin
who entered the mythology of Evil
with three billion dollars
to kill a child
to kill a forest of men.

The time has come for borrowed word
not to leave the abyss of our
sorrow
our faces have wrinkles as deep as the canyons
of Wadi Roum
and human bones litter
the streets of Beirut
mingled with animal refuse...
Let us name our children
Deir Yassin
Kalkilya

Sabra and
Shatila
lest we forget...

I never believed
that vengeance
would be a tree
growing in my garden

⸎

Trees grow in all directions
So do Palestinians:

uprooted
and unlike butterflies
wingless,
earthbound,
heavy with love
for their borders and their
misery,

no people can go forever behind
bars
or under the rain.

Their companions are the poets of
Russia and America
and the Indians from Guatemala...

O extinct volcanoes
where are your walls if not burned
and the fire that
eats mountains more bitterly
than the Deluge?!

We shall never cry with tears
but with blood.

When we created
the Angel of the Syrian Desert
he appeared dressed with
the Wind: there
were no leaves left on the dry bushes
of Arabia
so we called the flute player of
the Tribe

and asked him to
charm the waves of the Mediterranean:
she responded with a dirge.

We went to so many funerals
for so many years
that only the snow can
erase our footsteps

there is no snow in Jericho.

Ahmad and Muhammad
came knocking at the nuclear
door:
"let us save the world, they said
as an urgent task,
let us be insane."

There is no room for
anyone who is paperless in the
taxicabs of Beirut
and Ahmad has no name

Ahmad is blue like the banana trees from
Sidon
and yellow like the oranges grown
by his grandfather in Jaffa
But Muhammad is confused
he hallucinates

each night
in front of the radio
and vomits the news

Let us bury him with a long procession of
flowers.

Do you know?   Have you heard?
Did they tell you
that people were running in
the streets looking not for
their shoes but for
their feet?
not in a nightmare but in
front of television?

The sun is so strong in
Lebanon
that cameras were invisible...

Do you know? Did they tell you
that we grew elephant skins
on our eyes
and black hair behind the ears?

Oh how beautiful is the air between two clouds
over Mount Sannine
on October days!

but the slaughter happened in the dark

it took them three days and three nights
like the time Christ spent in the Tomb

Yes the Romans and the Jews
are waiting outside the
Great Wall of Sorrow
that surrounds the Palestinian shanty-towns

o refugees whose refuge
is not even
a
graveyard
but the dump site of the Eternal City:
the gutters of Beirut!

Let us not hurry to our
Doom
let us stop and look at the Sea.

I am speaking from the world of
the dead
while looking at the immaculate
beauty of the sky
our father

we know how thirsty summits are and the
dryness of the heart.

No language has words to describe
the human beast

we are not asking we are not
hoping

and after the news we took a bath and
shook hands with the weather.

I climbed the steps of Mount Tamalpais
with crutches
to look at the sunrise

but I fell into the open sewers of
Sabra and Shatila

A rosary of massacres for the Christian
monks of Lebanon
and the murders yet to come!

There are more people than insects
nowadays
and the pesticides are faltering
So
we shall go from one Final Solution to another
on the mad beaches of the Earth.

Let me warn you o clouds
they will shoot at you
too
because you are
better than we are

A pine tree stands at my door
like an angel of extermination
but I told him
he was guarding my ghost

The banana trees of Sidon
are blue and bruised
the enemy practiced tank
warfare
in the fields
to prevent the harvest and the Peace

Let us not forget the color
of the sea.

Poets go home
unless you change the world!

⁂

Blessed be those who fight
with their fists
against airplanes
Blessed be their weddings
and their tombs
Take my word for it:

We shall resurrect!

⁜

The sky is steel grey
as grey as warships
and the trees are desperately green
we are surrounded by a big
expanse of water
Divine Will does not speak with
fire and words anymore
it has deserted us long ago.

But Beirut under siege kept its
women dancing
yes
belly dancing
the mother belly
woman belly
kept its
honor alive
Beirut danced under a
shower of phosphorous bombs

the pride of the City was an Arab song.

The archaic sand dunes
of the land are on the march
again
mother-earth is a shroud

You left us with death-songs
but they are more beautiful
than your men

and left us under the rain with
knife-wounds in the belly
but a dead child from Ain Helweh

is worth fighting for
until your women spit
blood
in the River Jordan

It is not on cemeteries that we shall
plant grain
nor in the palm of my hand
We are as angry as a storm.

E. Ethelbert Miller

Dear Lebanon

I

Death
no longer waits for old age
it comes disguised as war

II

How can I continue to love
in a world which needs love
in a world where lovers pick bullets
from their hearts

my questions are flowers growing
in loneliness

to live in this world
without caring
is to be a poet
without voice or vision

to be uncommitted
is to show no mercy

Dear Lebanon
I bring you poems/prayers
& hymns

Sara Miles

From Bearsville to Palestine

Mountain laurel sassafras fox
grapes and lilies
still more trees than my tongue has room for pour
out oxygen day after day and I breathe
in deeply this day walking
thinking: homeland
past the old rock walls grown green with vine hearing
jets roar low over other
hills of home and it must be
almost night now in that land
where trees survive but breathing won't while
here beside the rushing water where a flat-leafed reed
pokes up
I wait for sunset thinking
homeland
where a heart was
and if the bombing has started yet.

Yasmin Adib

Memorandum

for Sabra and Shatila

"Never again"
they remind us.
"We must never forget"
the oppression
of our oppressors.
And they surround us
bearing lanterns
on a New Year's
sacrificial feast:
a festival of light.

"Never again"
will babies be borne
on trusted shoulders
to unsuspecting death,
they vow.
And their bright light
that leaves no shadow
snares a woman
shot in the back,
the baby
raised in her arms,
shot through the head:
a mother-child infantry
targeted in flight.

Their spotlight
on a firing line
of boyscouts
shot in uniform
without blindfolds,
cuts through the darkness.

And insects shield
the naked eyes

of a girl stunned
by the glare of the light
—stunned—
though they were used to
death
and had been warned.

"Never again."
The camp is crushed
by force this time—
not by endurance.
Arms are allotted
to lower levels.
Victory is viewed from tank tops
with lamplit halos.

"Never again"
they say
and shake their heads.
They 'mop up'
concentrations of bodies
with bulldozers.
(Oh yes,
I've seen holocaust footage.
Oh yes.
I'll never forget it.)

And back home.
Safe Haven secured,
they flash their light
accusingly
at the top.

"Never again"
will the world witness
genocide
in silence...
they pledge.
And the world
dumbfoundedly agrees.

Kathy Engel

A Time Comes When Silence Is Betrayal*

The tiniest birds dive
close overhead and rain
stirs the lake. A man
catches the same fish
three times. Does it say
in the Old Testament somewhere:
Kill your neighbors?

The quiet is unbearable
with you not here.
Instead of, or after
birth, the body's lining
gives itself up.
The same with death, I think.
In Arabic, the word poetry
comes from the root, to feel.
Poem is to aim.

Names of places and people
stick in the mouth like
grass rooted in the earth.
What they are doing in our names.
It takes a long time to count
the bodies, to count the dead.
A fish fin cuts
the shiney water like a knife.
Our only real weapon

is the heart and the howl
that comes from it.
Ordinary words
shred across the lake like fish scales.

I haven't learned the verb:
to-kill-in-great-numbers yet.
In November cars leave
places like this
with deer slung across the rooves.

The bodies are counted at tollbooths.
But in this promised land
living without guns
the deer have unlearned their fear.
They walk right up to the house.
And when a car's beaming lights
flash towards them at night,
they stop, transfixed in the road.

The news comes in French and British
papers: A flashlight in the door,
a man pulled in the road, a shot.
It happened before like that,
remember? Thousands scooped up
in a net and carried away.
In translation
the heart is cut out and saved.

Suddenly people died
who were gunned down.
Suddenly a massacre
is a surgical operation.
Suddenly your best friend
is foreign bacteria
to be cleansed, remember?
Suddenly there is a "logic

of invasion."
But it doesn't say that they
were sitting down to dinner.
That it was seven o'clock
and the youngest was playing

outside. That they were
like us, in love and looking
forward to a meal, sleep and

another day's work.
It doesn't say
they had names and habits,
hair and stains on their teeth.
It doesn't say
that they were there.

**This title is from a speech about the Vietnam War given by Dr. Martin Luther King, Jr.*

Gregory Orfalea

Pinecones

Scattered along the beach at Tyre
are thousands of pinecones
as if a conifer forest had tried
to seed the sea. Miracle of miracles—
there are no pines in Tyre.

Bits of gold cone glisten
in Phoenician sun—undoubtedly
Circe has come by and dropped
her jewelry. For there are
no rich people in Tyre.

From the sky they came these charms
of cone, from the steel sky
and innocent planes and no
wonder they had nowhere
to land in the ancient port

so thousands of parachutes of glittering
cone fell over the heads
of the people of Tyre
and it is no small feat
that no one is left in Tyre

that the pinecones are relaxing
on the sand
that one picked up
blows off the hand
burns the hair off the eyes.

The final miracle?
For these American pinecones
there are no eyes!

June Jordan

Moving Towards Home

"Where is Abu Fadi," she wailed. "Who will bring me my loved one?"
—New York Times, September 20, 1982

I do not wish to speak about the bulldozer and the red dirt
not quite covering all of the arms and legs
Nor do I wish to speak about
        the nightlong screams that reached
the observation posts where soldiers lounged about
Nor do I wish to speak about
        the woman who shoved her baby
into the stranger's hands before she was led away
Nor do I wish to speak about
        the father whose sons were shot
through the head while they slit his own throat before
        the eyes of his wife
Nor do I wish to speak about the army that lit continuous
flares into the darkness so that their flunkies could see
the backs of the victims lined against the wall
Nor do I wish to speak about
        the piled up bodies and the stench that will not float
Nor do I wish to speak about the nurse again and again raped
before they murdered her on the hospital floor
Nor do I wish to speak about the rattling bullets that did not
        halt on that keening trajectory
Nor do I wish to speak about the pounding on the doors and
the breaking of windows and the hauling of families into
the world of the dead
I do not wish to speak about the bulldozer and the red dirt
not quite covering all of the arms and legs
because I do not wish to speak about unspeakable events
that must follow from those who dare
"to purify" a people
those who dare
"to exterminate" a people
those who dare

to describe human beings as "beasts with two legs"
those who dare
"to mop up"
"to tighten the noose"
"to step up the military pressure"
"to ring around" civilian streets with tanks
those who dare
to close the universities
to abolish the press
to kill the elected representatives
of the people who refuse to be purified
those are the ones from whom we must redeem
the words of our beginning
the words of our god
because I need to speak about home
I need to speak about living room
where the land is not bullied and beaten into a tombstone
I need to speak about living room
where the talk will take place in my language
I need to speak about living room
where my children will grow without horror
I need to speak about living room where the men
of my family between the ages of six and sixty-five are not
marched into a roundup that leads to the grave
I need to talk about living room
where I can sit without grief without wailing aloud
for my loved ones
where I must not ask where is Abu Fadi
because he will be there beside me
I need to talk about living room
because I need to talk about home
I was born a Black woman
and now
I am become a Palestinian
against the relentless laughter of evil
there is less and less living room
and where are my loved ones?

It is time to make our way home

Gabrielle S. Edgcomb

Rosh Ha Shana 5743: The Days of Awe

I am not Israeli Zionist
Lebanese Palestinian
I'm German Jew
survivor from Berlin
before the last round-up

German Jew
tinder in the tinder box
tinder torched
to fuel the hellfire
German Jew is extinct

we never ran the Jewish state
our three disturbers of the sickening gods
died exiles
Marx Freud Einstein
tinders
the gods not buried yet

one of the handful of extinct survivors
I rage against all man made massacres

the crimes are re-enacted
there's no forgiving the shame
eternal people
eternal victim people
people of the book
bookish victim people
never again
superpower
why not
take the book on your vacation

the media single out as victims
women and children
I forgive them everything
the women and the children

after the hellfires
the news came lacerating us
sickening our full bellies
we were relieved to hear
that Tante Frieda died in bed
Theresinstadt
the ante-chamber
where young and old unfit for work
waited the journey
to the final shower

Tante Frieda died in bed
I remember her
at the piano in Berlin

but I had two Tante Friedas
my mother's sister died in bed
my father's sister
Tante Frieda
swallowed in the hellfire
without a trace

they're rounding up again
and still

Jane Creighton

Milagros

for Alana

Leg   *heart*   and *house*
I said to Alana
milagros for the Virgen de Guadalupe
which   I explained
are little pieces of the body
or home
cast in silver   presented by the faithful
for safekeeping
for cures

'It'll be a miracle'
like the child's Bible
the Ark's roseate curve
if you say
I can help
I can move hearts   the legs
and feet   dragging after

          always some
sunny   breach in the hills recurs
no war-torn youth   silly
belly   hands on my
heart   holding up atmospheric
body pressed into pine needles
on the floor of my forest

Alana
I was saying
your love for your friends
is a miracle of comprehension
and hope against
heroes who lead their people
into international ambush   What's
in a world?   *Leg*

heart and *house*   burning
in Beirut   like they have
elsewhere in time and for which
there are words like *martyrdom*
tragedy   *terrorist*   No body's
skin here but yours
and mine   friends contemplating miracles
of active rage against history
within memory's self
          Palestine
is your mother's early
Israeli self   Some version
out of the North Atlantic
belongs to mine
and someone else's mother
moves through the repertoire
of twisted steel   concrete
crumbling into bodies delivered
out of life   on the world's stage

They were not at home
where they said their hearts
belonged
                    Palestine
          insomniac   alive
is orchestrated into blood
despair   We grope in this
explosion of growth
which is not
what is?
optional

so that
I don't believe these words hanging
between us   or elsewhere
Beirut
I believe the miracle is
resistance   flesh with flesh
against fright

Sam Hamod

In Sabra

It is nothing, the blood
red   into black ground,   nothing,   we can say
nothing, the flares red and white, blue, nothing
against black sky, faces blur, nothing
sharp rope cuts into wrists, it is
nothing, slash of knife on throat, knowing
nothing, phalange, we hear the name phalange not
spoken, it is in the face. Haddad it is
nothing, mustache moves
nothing, these words
nothing, thunk of bazookas,   crunch
of bone, nothing, it is nothing, the
children run hiding under
the bed, like play, the man comes in
they say nothing, he laughs, tells them
they'll be safe, nothing, no sound, he
shouts "Come Out!" nothing
he lifts the bed
their big eyes open,
he laughs
his Uzi sputters
they are nothing
it is nothing
do not worry, they are
nothing, it is
nothing, do not worry, nothing
has happened
nothing, it is nothing, say it is nothing
be peaceful brothers and sisters do not run away
we will do nothing   it is nothing we do   nothing
it is nothing   nothing   nothing
oh, it is nothing
nothing at all
now say it and believe it, it is nothing
nothing   nothing
oh God   nothing

Kathy Engel

In the Middle of the Night in July

Fireflies grab the night
kissing the field of Queen Anne's Lace.
Stars shake and skid over the lake.
We don't have much time.
Unloading begins at the docks. Dreams first.
The moon guides the stragglers out,
spilling light over the water.
If you're not willing to give something up,
don't come here.

The dreams are mean
because they never stop.
Because they tell too much and someone
is always leaving. Because they are
always right. They are mean
because they are tireless and I tire
easily. Because they come back
and the untrustworthy come back
with candles and ammunition
and our language glistens in their mouths like razors.

Because they tell what but not
how. And my childhood friend appears
with her mother, cameras swinging, saying:
This isn't worth photographing.
This meeting, this memory lapse and lapse of love,
this eclipse. This tempest.
I can't iron but I can fold I repeat.
Who are you anyway, the dark-haired women in the corner asks.
What does it matter, I say, *we are trying*
to stop a war, isn't that what we're trying to do here?

The fish suck in air through their sides,
flip-flip, hooked and flung in a net.
Coyotes howl at the shifting light

and I think it's my own voice
escaping from dream.
I hear thunder and imagine: bombs.
I hear fireworks and imagine: bombs.
Across the lake, smoke; across the ocean,
borderlines, smoke. What I don't hear
I imagine.

Sparrows clip the treetops.
Clusters of leaves
hold the sky's breath in a cradle.
Harriet's laughter rows us safely to shore.
The moon returns orange.
We are beyond asking.
Now we must learn to invent.

June Jordan

The Cedar Trees of Lebanon

Bursting soft but kept by the structure of a spine
the green parts of the tree cloud under the clouds.
Under the axe the branches bleed red
dust. The tree bleeds red. The blood
of the cedar is red blood red body
enfolded by unmistakable brown skin.

At the end of this century massacre
remains invisible unless the victim
skin reads white.

Night air and the smoke from the chimney
puffs into a humid atmosphere obsessed
by particles from burned up cedar trees
a smell so defiantly sweet
the stars freeze to resist that violent and swollen
odor of a life transformed by fire.

At the end of this century massacre
becomes a cluster of phosphorus
events described by a woman carrying
a mattress on her head without
a destination.

At the end of this century a girl
stands her ground next to a tree
the Cedrus Libani
that the thunder does not shake
that the lightning cannot strike down

Dennis Lee

After Sabra, After Shatila

(I think of where death entered—
in the soft of the stomach for some;
for some at the hairline, just beside the temple. . .)

Source of our lives' own hunger,
if source there be:
the earth, our infinite planet
is growing small

and murder abounds.
Since time began
the bones of the harmless have slid, gone
crooked and splayed
in the shapes of unjust death—

since time began
though here, in this place,
in Canada
we scarcely know that thing, and it is
easy wisdom that would
set the far-off world to rights
while its own sheltered block slumps forward to neon ruin—

yet murder does abound.
The planet grows smaller, and
camps in Lebanon are
clogged with the stink of humans, dead.
And if we gag, if we reach for hard judgments, if we
call to other men, Stop:
punish the killers, and end this obscenity,

it is that harmless lives have been splayed too long, and in a
cross-hatch of agony those

children watched their parents disintegrate
and then their own uncomprehending bodies
fell—the bullet entering the stomach perhaps,
or else beside the temple, just at the hairline,
and the child was four, pretty soon he would
pat the dog next
door, he *knew* he'd be brave enough soon-
entering just at the hairline—perhaps in the soft of
the stomach—
ending their lives' own hungers. . .

Source of all living hunger,
whatever you be—
there is no
easy dream of peace that will not
founder. The harmless will go on dying, with a broken
constancy. Our own green planet, sweet
mother in space, may come apart,
one tiny popped balloon in the intergalactic silence
for murder abounds.
Yet as the earth grows smaller now and restive in its turning, as
we jostle, even in sleep, with bodies halfway round
the globe,
it is time—time that the race
of the beings who dwell on earth
imagine their death.

Imagine our death:
not me, not yours, not a city alone, not one more animal
species gone down, not just a
continent: the race of the
beings of earth, all hale and quick or crippled plants &
sapiens, no
exit no reprieve all gone utterly, finis the
billion years of—

the imagination falters.
Yet I know one thing: the butchers of Sabra

must come to law.
Not to satisfy us, with our deadline media wisdom.
Not to simplify things for us, who never lived
where the whiplash of hate has snaked through
generations, changing
the very texture of *shelter, tomorrow, friend*.
And least of all to keep us safe in the dream
of a cozy brotherhood of all mankind
where the sight of blood is a squeamish aberration.

And though I grieve on my nerve-ends for
all those butchered and bulldozed,
they cannot use my grief.
Though I gawk in rage at the simple thought of
their killers, I
cannot help to track them down.
But here, on a small planet
that moves through the forward shadow of extinction,
there is no choice now.
We must reckon, with butchers.
They must be brought to law, for now at last
the law must be brought to earth.

For we are one race, or gone—not by
choice, not by
liking nor folkways nor will,
yet we *are*
one race: the race of beings
that will perish together if planet earth is destroyed,
and if Sabra prevails
the story of Sabra will be the story of earth.

(. . .I think of where death entered—
in the soft of the stomach for some;
for some at the hairline, very close to the temple. . .)

If we mean to continue,
continue existing on earth,

we need not love one another.
But we must draw together, and know our enemies
for there are things that are no longer
acceptable,
if the planet is not to go down.

Our enemies are those who do not recognize
our painful, shared community.
We must know them well,
after Sabra. . .
after Shatila. . .

Sara Miles

My Humanitarian Response to the War in Lebanon

Talking about tragedy we drive
north on gravel roads cold
clearings where fir
blurs the blue lake's
edges. Where in all this
wilderness could I hide my rage? The war
isn't tragic. It's wrong.

I could pull into the lonely
diner, or not: swerve to avoid
the terrified woodchuck or narrow
my eyes to the hot fur suddenly
under the tires.
There are fires; there are floods
there are blizzards and bloodchilling
thunder but I make
tragedy, or don't.
It happens like accidents
do. They don't.

Once you said, pitiless. Then
later, forgive: as in, it's hard
to forgive. I watch the Adirondacks
swelling into summer; black hawks
swooping out of thin air where
it's easy to forget
our day will come: our tragic death
by avalanche
from the exact and waiting volcano
where we tried to hide and bury wrong.

Kathy Engel

Life Support

for Sara, June, Viv

Ashes rise out of ashes.
A sound of wailing throws itself
over the earth
like a woman's shawl.
Who can witness their own deaths
and survive to build a home
out of the nothing that is left.
the nothing that was there?

A putrid flame
crawls over this small child,
her voice smothered in mud
calling in an ancient language
to her mother, falling, to her father.
falling and twisted over the sacks
of flesh that are no longer human bodies,
her hair matted across her eyes and nose and mouth,
arms caked with red and dirt,
her fingernails, small blood-filled shells,
arms waving before her.

We watch
on the television screen
as the camera pulls back
and the screams follow
switching channels incessantly
to get each news on each station
with each commentator
with combed hair and the language of war
the language of rationale
many numbers and no names
as the child is dragged into the street,

tent flap stripped open,
where is her name?

We turn on the radio
buy newspapers from other cities
clip out column after column
till we could paper our walls
with newsprint
and we call each other on the phone,
how are you, how are you, how are you,
as though we had a grammar
that could reach across those wires
and tell us what to do.

We can't get close enough
pushing our faces up against the smudged
screen, turning from ABC to CBS to NBC.
One fly buzzes across the cool surface
and there—flies upon flies swarm,
the voices of foreign correspondents and political
  representatives:
    we don't know exactly when
    we don't know exactly how many
    we don't know exactly who
    we don't know exactly who to blame
but we know what to call it
done in this way on the ground
out of the wedlock of official arms:
Massacre. Massacre.
Before, in the green burst of June,
that birth month, and in the hot
summer, in the sweating days,
they had no faces
when there were planes and tanks
and shells shattering.

And we can't push our faces into the screen
through the static

to be there, to cup
our warm safe faraway American hands
over the child's eyes and stroke her face
and say something none of us could understand.

It is too late after the evening news
to call the White House, the Senator,
too late to call a meeting or signers
for a newspaper ad, too late to suck out the
bullet from the mother's chest,
sew together the man's belly,
too late to build a home around the crumpled homeless bodies
to give them, finally, in their deaths
a place of their own, to give the child back
her sister and brother strewn like broken furniture.

It is too late to forgive
on this eve, this night
of atonement, this Yom Kippur,
too late to gather up forgiveness
the way they gathered flowers
that grew out of the bombed city's rubble
where cement and bricks crumbled
and they made wreaths
for the men to wear
on their heads as they walked out of that city
away from all they had and who they loved.

Where are the names of those
who had no home
and died, unburied, without a stone?

Let us write them down, one by one.
Let us recite them
in our sleepless hours
in our locked apartments
in this American city
where we call each other

and look into the eyes of the sisters and brothers and cousins
of those who died
and hold them.
I call my friends twelve times a day:
I could dial the numbers in the dark.
We remind each other:
It begins here,
with this caring, this
fullness of care.

Samuel Hazo

The Color of Reluctance

September, and the wild apple
bowls its harvests down
our drive.
By ones the apples
wabble to a rot-halt
before I pitch them to the woods.
If "ripeness is all," I've had
Too much of *all*.
The apples
disagree and church me
to their creed.
"Why rush?
Winter will claim us soon
enough.
We've weathered
lightning and the blight.
Slow
Deaths are all we ask."
Before they turn to sentinels
the trees in all their leafy
languages agree.
From green
to cinnamon to blood to beige
to brittle, they make the case
for slowness. . .
Slow as a wound. . .
Slow as the breath of sleepers. . .
They stand opposed to all
that ended all at once in Sabra
and Shatila and the South of France.
"Help us!
"They're killing
everybody."
"I'm sad and empty,
Sam.

You know how the Princess
was nice."
Unsuddenly as fall
the apples bounce and dribble
to their rest like balls.
They speak
for dying young when you're
as old as possible despite
the wind, despite the worst.
The last, high apple never falls.

Credits

Thanks to all contributing poets who allowed us to reprint their poems originally appearing in *And Not Surrender: American Poets on Lebanon*; and to all those who granted us permission to include their poems in this anthology. The majority of poems included here are appearing for the first time. A few have appeared online. Poems that have either been published or are scheduled to appear in publications after this volume goes to press are:

Ammiel Alcalay
"[I moved as free as light]" and "[In this our day of darkness]." From *from the warring factions* (Venice, CA: Beyond Baroque Books, 2002).

Seema V. Atalla
"Gift." From *Banipal*, no.10/11 (spring/summer, 2001).
"Holy Land." From *Banipal*, no. 4 (spring, 1999).

Robert Bagg
"Yeah" and "Bumper Sticker Blues." From *Niké and Other Poems*, 2nd revised printing (Washington, D.C.: Azul Editions, 2006).

John Balaban
"Ibn Fadhlan, the Arab Emissary, Encounters Vikings on the Volga River, 922 A.D." From *Path, Crooked Path* (Port Townsend, WA: Copper Canyon Press, 2006).

Sarah Browning
"Sunday Outing With Yellow Leaves" and "Sunday Morning, Spring." From *D.C. Poets Against the War*. Edited by Sarah Browning, Michelle Elliot, and Danny Rose (Washington, D.C.: the Argonne House Press, 2004).

Dennis Brutus
"[In this time]" and "[Exile]." From *Poetry & Protest: A Dennis Brutus Reader*. Edited by Lee Sustar and Aisha Karim (Chicago: Haymarket Books, 2006).

Reja-e Busailah
"In the Shadow of the Holy Heights." From *Aura Literary/Arts Review*, (University of Alabama at Birmingham) 25 (fall/winter 1988), and in *Anemone* (Chester, Vermont), no. 9 (summer 1988).

Grace Cavalieri
"Fateema." From *D.C. Poets Against the War*. Edited by Sarah Browning, Michelle Elliot, and Danny Rose (Washington, D.C.: the Argonne House Press, 2004).

"How a Poem Begins." From *Cuffed Frays and Other Poems* (Washington D.C.: Argonne House Press, 2001), and in *Water on the Sun* (Boca Raton, FL: Bordighera Press, 2006).
"War Theater" from *Poems Against War 5* (Baltimore, MD, 2006).

Hayan Charara
"Lucy." To be published in *Michigan Quarterly Review*, 2006.

Ariel Dorfman
"Hammurabi, the Exalted Prince Who Made Great the Name of Babylon, has Words From the Other Side of Death for Donald Rumsfeld." From *Other Septembers, Many Americas* (New York: Seven Stories Press, 2005).

Martín Espada
"Between the Rockets and the Songs," "The God of the Weather-Beaten Face," and "Blues for the Soldiers Who Told You." From *The Republic of Poetry* (New York: W.W. Norton, 2006).

Wade Fletcher
"Unmovable." From *D.C. Poets Against the War*. Edited by Sarah Browning, Michelle Elliot, and Danny Rose (Washington, D.C.: the Argonne House Press, 2004).

Margaret Gibson
"Fuel" and "Moment." From *Iowa Review*, 2006. Also to be published in *One Body*. Reprinted by permission of Louisiana State University Press copyright © 2007 by Margaret Gibson.

Sam Hamill
"Eyes Wide Open" from *Rattle*, no. 24 (winter 2005). "Homeland Security." To be published in *Measured by Stone* (Willimantic, CT: Curbstone Press, 2007).

Joy Harjo
"Equinox." From *How We Became Human: New and Selected Poems* (New York: W.W. Norton, 2002).

Samuel Hazo
"Intifada." From *Just Once: New and Selected Poems* (Pittsburgh, PA: Autumn House Press, 2002)
"For Which It Stands." From *A Flight to Elsewhere* (Pittsburgh, PA: Autumn House Press, 2005).

June Jordan
"Apologies to all the People in Lebanon," "To Sing a Song of

Palestine," "Moving Towards Home," and "The Cedar Trees of Lebanon." From *And Not Surrender: American Poets on Lebanon*. Edited by Kamal Boullata (Washington, D.C.: Arab American Cultural Foundation, 1982). Copyright 2006 June M. Jordan Literary Estate Trust: reprinted by permission.

Melanie Kaye/Kantrowitz

"Jerusalem Shadow." From *The Tribe of Dina: A Jewish Woman's Anthology*. Edited by Melanie Kaye/Kantrowitz and Irena Klepfisz (Boston: Beacon Press, 1989). Reprinted in *Looking for Home: Women Writing About Exile*. Edited by Deborah Keenan and Roseann Lloyd (Minneapolis: Milkweed Editions, 1990).

Denise Levertov

"Perhaps No Poem But All I Can Say and I Cannot Be Silent." From *And Not Surrender: American Poets on Lebanon*. Edited by Kamal Boullata (Washington, D.C.: Arab American Cultural Foundation, 1982). Reprinted by permission of New Directions Publishing Corp.

Lisa Suhair Majaj

"The Coffin Maker Speaks." From *World Literature Today* 80, no. 6, (2006).

"Fifty Years On/Stones in an Unfinished Wall." From *Ripe Guava: Voices of Women of Color* (fall 1999–spring 2000).

D.H. Melhem

"Boy in a Hospital." From *Conversation with a Stonemason* (New York: IKON, 2003).

W.S. Merwin

"Ash." From *Migration: New and Selected Poems* (Port Townsend, WA: Copper Canyon Press, 2005).

E. Ethelbert Miller

"There are Oceans Left to Kill." From *Dance the Guns to Silence*. Edited by Nii Ayikwei Parkes, Kadija Sessay, and Kadija George (London: Flipped Eye Press, 2005).

Naomi Shihab Nye

"Letters My Prez is not Sending." To be published in *Court Green*, 2007.

Frank Reeve

"The Blue Cat Writes to His Cousin in Baghdad." To be published in *Marlboro Review* (spring 2007).

Adrienne Rich

"The School Among the Ruins." From *The School Among the Ruins: Poems 2000–2004* (New York: W.W. Norton, 2004).

Sonia Sanchez

"Peace." From *Dance the Guns to Silence*. Edited by Nii Ayikwei Parkes, Kadija Sessay, and Kadija George (London: Flipped Eye Press, 2005).

Richard Schaff

Earlier versions of "In Mosul" and "No Natural Disaster" were published in *Nimrod International Journal* 49, no. 2 (spring 2006).

James Scully

"Qana," "Donatello's Version," "Dadalab," and "Boxcars." To be published in *Donatello's Version* (Willimantic, CT: Curbstone Press, April 2007).

Andy Young

"Thinking of Rasha." From *Mizna* 8, issue 2 (December 2006).

Every effort has been made to contact all rights holders. Appropriate credit will gladly be run in the next printing of this book should the rights holder be made known to the publisher.

Contributors

Elmaz Abinader is a poet, writer, and activist. Her books include *Children of the Roojme: A Family Journey from Lebanon* (1991) and *In the Country of My Dreams* (1999) for which she received the Josephine Miles PEN Oakland Award. The recipient of numerous awards, including two Drammy Awards for her performance of *Country of My Origin*, she currently teaches at Mills College in Oakland.

Yasmin Adib is a poet and activist. Her poems have appeared in *Woman of Power*, *The Returning Woman*, and *MADRE Newsletter*. She has also published articles in *City Limits* and in *Newsday*. She is currently working as Development Coordinator for Al-Bustan Seeds of Culture in Philadelphia.

Etel Adnan is a painter, poet, and playwright whose writings have been widely anthologized and translated to different languages. Her latest works are *There* (1997), *In/somnia* (2002), and *In the Heart of the Heart of Another Country* (2006). She lives in California, with frequent visits to Paris and Beirut.

Saladin Ahmed was born in Detroit. His work appeared in various journals and in the anthologies *Post-Gibran: New Arab American Writing*, edited by Khaled Mattawa and Munir Akash (2000), and *Abandon Automobile: Detroit City Poetry*, edited by Melba J. Boyd and M.L. Liebler (2001).

Ammiel Alcalay is a poet, translator, critical scholar, and activist whose recent work includes *Scrapmetal* (2007), and *A Little History* (2007). Alcalay's other books include *After Jews and Arabs* (1993), *Keys to the Garden* (1996), *Memories of Our Future* (1999), and *from the warring factions* (2002). He teaches at Queens College and the Graduate Center of the City University of New York.

Seema V. Atalla currently writes, translates, and teaches in southern California. Her poetry and translations have appeared in several journals and anthologies, including *A Crack in the Wall: New Arab Poetry*, edited by Margaret Obank and Samuel Shimon (2001), and *The Poetry of Arab Women: A Contemporary Anthology*, edited by Nathalie Handal (2001).

Robert Bagg's most recent books are *Niké and Other Poems* (2006) and *The Oedipus Plays of Sophocles* (2004), the latter co-authored with his wife, Mary Bagg. They are currently researching a critical biography of Richard Wilbur, for which he has been awarded a Fellowship from the National Endowment for the Humanities. With James Scully, he is translating the non-Oedipus plays of Sophocles.

John Balaban is the author of twelve books of poetry and prose. His awards include the Academy of American Poets' Lamont prize, and a National Poetry Series Selection. His *Locusts at the Edge of Summer: New and Selected Poems* won the 1998 William Carlos Williams Award from the Poetry Society of America. He is also a translator of Vietnamese poetry.

Amiri Baraka is a writer of poetry, drama, essays, and music criticism and a social critic and activist. Poet Laureate of the State of New Jersey, he has won numerous awards, including, in 1983, an American Book Award with Amina Baraka for *Confirmation: An Anthology of African-American Women*, the PEN/Faulkner Award, the Rockefeller Award for Drama, and a Langston Hughes Award.

John Berger is a painter and writer. His works include novels, short stories, poetry, critical studies in art and contemporary culture. In 1972 he won the Booker Prize for fiction for his novel *G*, and he scripted the BBC's groundbreaking series on art, *Ways of Seeing*. His most recent publications include *The Shape of a Pocket* (2002) and *Here is Where We Meet* (2005).

Barbara Berman reviews poetry for the Book Review of the *San Francisco Chronicle* and is on the jury of the California Book Awards. Her prose and poetry have appeared in the *Village Voice*, *Lilith*, *Asian Week*, *Coracle*, and elsewhere. She is at work on a prose book, *Meditations of a Liberal Catholic Convert*.

Kamal Boullata is a painter and writer. He is the author of *Recovery of Place: A Study of Contemporary Palestinian Art* (in Arabic, 2001), *Palestinian Art: Discontinuities and Resistance, 1845–2005* (forthcoming), and is the editor of *Belonging and Globalisation: Critical Essays in Contemporary Art and Culture* (2007). Poetry collections he has translated and edited include *Women of the Fertile Crescent: Modern Poetry by Arab Women* (1978, 1994). With Mirène Ghossein he co-edited *The World of Rashed Hussein: A Palestinian Poet in Exile* (1978) and *If Only the Sea Could Sleep: Love Poems by Adonis* (2003).

Sarah Browning is co-editor of *D.C. Poets Against the War: An Anthology* (2004) and coordinates the group of the same name. The recipient of a People Before Profits Poetry Prize, she is currently organizing a festival of poetry of witness, to be held in Washington, D.C., in March 2008.

Dennis Brutus, a poet and teacher who was imprisoned along with Nelson Mandela, was honored with the first Paul Robeson Award in 1989 for "artistic excellence, political consciousness and integrity." He is currently a professor of African Studies and African Literature and chair of the Department of Black Community Education Research and Development at the University of Pittsburgh.

Reja-e Busailah is the author of a collection of poems, *We Are Human* (1985). His poetry has appeared in *The Ordeal* (1978) and in journals, including *Arab Studies Quarterly*. Born in Jerusalem and educated in Cairo and New York, he founded a school for the blind in Kuwait. He is a retired professor from the University of Indiana and is currently working on his childhood memoir.

Grace Cavalieri is the author of 14 books of poetry, 20 plays, and produced "The Poet and the Poem" on public radio for 29 years. Her honors include the Allen Ginsburg Award for Poetry, a Paterson Prize for Poetry, the Pen Syndicated Fiction Award, the Bordighera Poetry Award, the Folger's "Columbia Award," and CPB's Silver Medal. Her latest book, *What I Would Do For Love: Poems in the Voice of Mary Wollstonecraft, 1759–1797* (2004), is the basis for her new play, "Hyena in Petticoats."

Hayan Charara is a teacher, author, and poet whose published work includes a collection of poems, *The Alchemist's Diary* (2001). His poems appeared in the *Kenyon Review* and in *Post-Gibran: Anthology of New Arab American Writing*, edited by Khaled Mattawa and Munir Akash (2000). He is currently working on a novel entitled *The Mythology of Love and Hate*. Since 1994, he has edited the annual literary anthology *Graffiti Rag*.

Jane Creighton teaches American literature and creative writing at the University of Houston–Downtown, where she also serves as director of the Cultural Enrichment Center. Her writings have appeared in *Ploughshares*, the *American Voice*, and *Gulf Coast*, and in the anthologies *Unwinding the Vietnam War*, edited by Reese Williams

(1987), and *Close to the Bone: Memoirs of Hurt, Rage, and Desire,* edited by Laurie Stone (1998).

Alexis De Veaux is a poet, fiction writer, playwright, essayist, and biographer, whose books include *Don't Explain: A Song of Billie Holiday* (1980), and *An Enchanted Hair Tale* (1987), for which she received a Coretta Scott King Award. She has won several prestigious awards for her acclaimed biography of Audre Lorde, *Warrior Poet* (2004), including the Zora Neale Hurston/Richard Wright Foundation Legacy Award. She is associate professor in the Department of Women's Studies at SUNY Buffalo.

Ariel Dorfman is a poet, novelist, playwright, essayist, translator, and journalist. He has just published *The Burning City* (2006), a novel he wrote with his youngest son, Joaquin; and *Exorcising Terror: The Incredible Unending Trial of General Augusto Pinochet* (2002). He holds the Walter Hines Page Chair of Literature and Latin American Studies at Duke University.

Gabrielle Edgcomb (1920–1997) published her poetry in numerous periodicals, including *Off Our Backs*, *Woodwind*, and *Washington Review for the Art.* The editor of *Working Cultures,* she was the author of the collection *Moving Violations* (1973) and *From Swastika to Jim Crow: Refugee Scholars at Black Colleges* (1993), the basis of the PBS documentary. She also translated from German *Marx and Suicide* (1993), edited by E.A. Plaut and K. Anderson.

Kathy Engel is a poet, teacher, producer, and consultant for social justice and peace organizations. She is the author of two collections: *Banish the Tentative* (1989) and *Ruth's Skirts* (2007). She serves on the advisory board of the U.S. Campaign to End the Israeli Occupation.

Martín Espada is the author of several collections of poetry, most recently *The Republic of Poetry* (2006) and *Alabanza: New and Selected Poems: 1982–2002* (2003). The recipient of an American Book Award for his collection *Imagine the Angels of Bread* (1996), he is a professor in the Department of English at the University of Massachusetts–Amherst, where he teaches creative writing, Latino poetry, and the work of Pablo Neruda.

Lawrence Ferlinghetti is San Francisco's first poet laureate (1998) and the co-founder of City Lights Publishing. A poet and a painter, he has also translated the work of Nicanor Parra, Jacques Prévert, and Pier Paolo Pasolini. In 2003 he was awarded the Robert Frost Memorial Medal, the Authors' Guild Lifetime Achievement Award, and he was elected to the prestigious American Academy of Arts and Letters.

Wade Fletcher organizes around various social justice issues and helps run the Brian MacKenzie Infoshop, a radical bookstore and resource center, in Washington, D.C.

Margaret Gibson's collections include *Long Walks in the Afternoon*, the 1982 Lamont Selection of the Academy of American Poets; and *The Vigil* (1993), a finalist for the National Book Award. She has been awarded two Pushcart Prizes, the James W. Boatwright Prize, and the Melville Cane Award of the Poetry Society of America. She is a visiting professor at the University of Connecticut.

Sam Hamill has written fourteen volumes of poetry, three collections of essays, and been translated into more than a dozen languages. Founder and editor of *Poets Against the War* (2003), he is the co-founder of Copper Canyon Press and received the Stanley Lindberg Lifetime Achievement Award for Editing and the Washington Poets Association Lifetime Achievement Award.

Suheir Hammad is the author of *Born Palestinian, Born Black* (1996), *Drops of This Story* (1996), and *ZaatarDiva* (2006). The co-writer and performer of the Tony award-winning "Russell Simmons Def Poetry Jam on Broadway," Hammad has also written the libretto for *Blood Trinity* (2002) and *Re-Orientalism* (2003). She has performed her poetry in many countries and her work has been widely anthologized. She is the granddaughter of 1948 Palestinian refugees.

Sam Hamod is the author of *Dying with the Wrong Name* (1980). He has published ten collections of poetry, the most recent of which are *The Arab Poems, The Muslim Poems* (2000), and *Just Love Poems For You,* (2006). His poetry appeared in numerous anthologies. He has taught at the Writers Workshop of the University of Iowa, and at Princeton, Michigan, and Howard.

Nathalie Handal is poet, writer and playwright. Her most recent books include, *The Neverfield* (2005); *The Lives of Rain* (2005), which was short-listed for the Agnes Lynch Starrett Poetry Prize/The Pitt Poetry Series; and *Spell* (2006). She is the editor of *Arab-American and*

Arab Anglophone Literature and co-editor of *Contemporary Poetry of the Eastern World: An Anthology of Poems,* both of which are forthcoming in 2007. She teaches at Columbia University.

Joy Harjo is a poet, teacher, jazz saxophonist, and author of ten books, most recently *How We Became Human* (2002). She co-edited the anthology *Reinventing the Enemies' Language* (1998). Her honors include a Lifetime Achievement Award from the National Endowment for the Arts. She lives in Hawaii and travels frequently giving poetry readings with her band, Poetic Justice.

Samuel Hazo is the author of poetry, fiction, essays, and plays, and founder and director of the International Poetry Forum in Pittsburgh, Pennsylvania. He is also McAnulty Distinguished Professor of English emeritus at Duquesne, where he taught for 43 years. The recipient of Notre Dame's Griffin Award for Creative Writing, he was the first state poet of Pennsylvania, where he served from 1993 to 2003. His book *Just Once: New and Previous Poems* (1999) received the Maurice English Poetry Award in 2003.

Jack Hirschman is a poet, painter, translator, and social activist, who was appointed San Francisco's poet laureate in 2006. He has written more than 50 volumes of poetry and essays, including *The Bottom Line* (1988) and *Endless Threshold* (1992). He has published translations of poetry from eight languages and assists in the editing of *Left Curve* and is a correspondent for the *People's Tribune.*

Rashidah Ismaili writes short stories, plays, and poetry. Her work has appeared in different anthologies and she has published four poetry collections. Her play *Rice Keepers* (2006) was presented in a staged reading as part of the "Ebony States," in the American Museum's annual African-American History Month celebration.

Gale Jackson is a poet and cultural historian who received a National Endowment for the Arts fellowship for her work in Griot traditions. Her books include *Bridge Suite: Narrative Poems* (1998), *A Khoisan Tale of Beginnings and Ends* (1998), *MeDea* (2005), and *Suite for Mozambique* (2005). She is a poet in residence at the Secondary School for Journalism and a storyteller in residence at the Hayground School.

June Jordan (1936–2002) was a poet, activist, teacher, and writer. Her books of poetry include *Haruko/Love Poems* (1994), *Kissing God*

Goodbye: Poems 1991–1997 (1997), and her posthumously published collection of poems *Directed by Desire* (2005). Her collected essays appeared under the title *Some of Us Did not Die* (2002). She received the National Association of Black Journalists' Award and taught at the University of California at Berkeley, where she founded Poetry for the People.

Melanie Kaye/Kantrowitz is an activist, writer, and scholar, whose books include *My Jewish Face & Other Stories* (1990), *The Issue Is Power: Essays on Women, Jews, Violence and Resistance* (1992), and *The Colors of Jews: Racial Politic and Radical Diasporism,* forthcoming in 2007. She teaches comparative literature at Queens College and with the Bard College Prison Initiative.

Naomi Lazard is the author of several collections of poetry, including *Cry of the Peacocks* (1975), *The Moonlight Upper Deckerina* (1977), and *Ordinances* (1990). Her poems have appeared in the *American Poetry Review,* the *Nation, Harpers,* and the *New Yorker.*

Dennis Lee was born in Toronto, Canada. He has published more than twenty poetry collections for adults and children; he is also an essayist, song lyricist, and editor. From 2001 to 2004 he was Toronto's first poet laureate. His most recent collection, *Yesno,* is forthcoming in 2007.

Denise Levertov (1923–1997) published more than twenty volumes of poetry, including *Freeing the Dust* (1975), which won the Lenore Marshall Poetry Prize. She was also the author of four books of prose, translator of three volumes of poetry, and taught at Stanford University.

Kathryn Levy is the author of *Losing the Moon* (2006). Her poetry and reviews have appeared in *Provincetown Arts,* the *Manhattan Poetry Review, Blink,* the *East Hampton Star,* and the *Light of City and Sea.* She was founding director of the Poetry Exchange and the New York City Ballet Poetry Project, two poetry-in-the-schools organizations.

Chris Llewellyn is a poet and painter. Winner of the Academy of American Poets' Walt Whitman Award for her *Fragments From the Fire* (1987), she has taught poetry workshops in elementary schools, colleges, prisons, and for adults and children at the Writers' Center in Bethesda, Maryland. Author of *Steam Dummy* (1993), she has been published in numerous anthologies and periodicals.

Lisa Suhair Majaj's poetry has appeared in *Food For Our Grandmothers: Writings by Arab-American and Arab-Canadian Feminists*, edited by Joanna Kadi (1994), and in *Miscegenation Blues: Voices of Mixed Race Women*, edited by Carol Camper (1994). Her awards include the Worcester County Poetry Association fourth prize in 1989 and the New England Poetry Club's Best Published Poem in 1995. She is co-editor of *Going Global: The Transnational Reception of Third World Women* (2000).

Khaled Mattawa is a poet and translator. His poetry collections include *Ismailia Eclipse* (1995) and *Zodiac of Echoes* (2003). His poetry has appeared in numerous journals, including *Poetry*, the *Kenyon Review*, *New England Review,* and the *Pushcart Prize* anthology. The translator of three volumes of Arabic poetry, he is the recipient of an Academy of American Poets' Award. Currently, he is professor of English and creative writing at California State University, Northridge.

Pablo Medina has written ten books of poetry and prose, most recently a novel, *The Cigar Roller* (2005), and a bilingual collection of poetry, *Points of Balance/Puntos de apoyo* (2005). He is currently working with poet Mark Statman on a new English version of *Poet in New York* by Federico García Lorca, to be published in 2008. He is visiting professor at the University of Nevada, Las Vegas.

D.H. Melhem is a poet, novelist, scholar, and essayist whose writings include two anthologies, the musical drama *Children of the House Afire* (1976), the novel *Blight* (2003), and the collection *New York Poems* (2005). Her numerous awards for poetry and prose include an American Book Award. She is vice president of the International Women's Writing Guild.

W.S. Merwin's first book of poems won the Yale Series of Younger Poets Award for 1952. He went on to write *The Carrier of Ladders* (1970), which received a Pulitzer Prize, *The River Sound* (1999), which was named a New York Times Notable Book of the Year, and *Migration,* which won the 2005 National Book Award. He is the author of more than 50 books of poetry and 20 translated works, including Dante's *Purgatorio.*

Sara Miles is a writer living in San Francisco.

E. Ethelbert Miller, the board chair of the Institute for Policy Studies, was the chair of the Humanities Council of Washington,

D.C. and a core faculty member of the Bennington Writing Seminars. The "D.C. We Read" program selected his memoir, *Fathering Words: The Making of an African American Writer* (2000), as the book all Washingtonians were encouraged to read.

Tracie Morris is the author of two poetry collections, *Chap-T-her Woman* (1993) and *Intermission* (1998). Her awards include the National Haiku Slam Championship and an Asian Cultural Council Fellowship.

Naomi Shihab Nye has written numerous books of poetry, including *You and Yours* (2005), which received the Isabella Gardner Poetry Award, and *19 Varieties of Gazelle: Poems of the Middle East* (2002). She has received awards from the Texas Institute of Letters, the Carity Randall Prize, the International Poetry Forum, as well as four Pushcart Prizes. She has been a Lannan Fellow, a Guggenheim Fellow, and a Wittner Bynner Fellow.

Gregory Orfalea is the author of *The Arab Americans: A History* (2006). He has published six other books of creative nonfiction, history, and poetry. He is director of the Pitzer College Center for Writing.

Frank Reeve is a poet, novelist, literary critic, and translator. His collections include *Moon and Other Failures* (1999), *The Toy Soldiers* (2006), and *The Puzzle Master* (2006), in collaboration with composer Eric Chasalow. His travelogue *Robert Frost in Russia* (1962, 2001) documents his USSR trip with Frost. The translator of over a dozen books from Russian literature, his most recent is Leonid Andreyev's *A Story About Seven Who Were Hanged*. The recipient of the Golden Rose for lifelong poetic achievement, his presentations with jazz include *The Blue Cat Walks the Earth*.

Adrienne Rich received the Yale Series of Younger Poets prize for her first book *A Change of World* (1951) and the National Book Award for *Diving Into the Wreck* (1973). She has won countless honors, including the Bollingen Prize, the Lannan Lifetime Achievement Award, the Ruth Lilly Poetry Prize, and the American Academy of Poets' Wallace Stevens Award.

Sonia Sanchez is a poet, activist, professor, essayist, and playwright, a key figure in the Black Arts Movement, who has edited anthologies on black literature and has published more than seventeen books of poetry, including *Does Your House Have Lions?* (1998) and *Shake Loose My*

Skin (2000). The recipient of many awards, she was the first African-American woman to receive the Frost Medal from the Poetry Society of America.

Richard Schaaf has published a volume of his poetry, *Revolutionary at Home* (1975), and has translated or co-translated fifteen books of Latin American literature, including works by César Vallejo, Pablo Neruda, Roque Dalton, and Leonel Rugama. He is the founding editor of Azul Editions, an independent literary press devoted to publishing socially and politically engaged literature.

James Scully has published poetry, essays, plays, and translations. The recipient of a Lamont Award for his first book of poems, *The Marches* (1967), his collections include *Santiago Poems* (1975), *Scrap Book* (1977), *May Day* (1980), and *Apollo Helmet* (1983). Recently Curbstone Press has re-issued the out-of-print essays of his *Line Break: Poetry As Social Practice* (1988, 2005) and a collection of new poems, *Donatello's Version* (2007). His translations include Aeschylus' *Prometheus Bound* (1975).

Susan Sherman is a poet, playwright, and editor of IKON magazine. She has published three collections of poetry, a translation, and *The Color of the Heart: Writing from Struggle & Change, 1959–1990* (1990). Recent awards include 1990 and 1997 New York Foundation for the Arts fellowships and a Puffin Foundation Grant. Her book *America's Child: A Personal Chronicle of the Radical 60s* is forthcoming from Curbstone Press, 2007.

Becky Thompson is a poet, writer, and teacher, whose poems have recently appeared in *Warpland: A Journal of Black Literature, Ideas, Amandla, Illuminations*, and *In Women's Hands*. Her poetry collections include *A Hunger So Wide and So Deep* (1994), *Mothering Without a Compass* (2000), and *A Promise and a Way of Life* (2001).

Andy Young is the co-editor of *Meena* magazine, a bilingual Arabic-English literary journal, and is the director of creative writing at the New Orleans Center for Creative Arts. Her poems, essays, and translations are forthcoming in *third coast*, *Southern Quarterly*, and in *Contemporary Voices from the Eastern World*, edited by Tina Chang, Nathalie Handal, and Ravi Shankar (2007).